I'm Not
WONDER
WOMAN

I'm Not
WONDER
WOMAN
But God Made Me
Wonderful!

Sheila Walsh

THOMAS NELSON
Since 1798

NASHVILLE   DALLAS   MEXICO CITY   RIO DE JANEIRO   BEIJING

Published in Nashville, Tennessee, by Thomas Nelson. Thomas Nelson is a registered trademark of Thomas Nelson, Inc.

Published in association with Yates & Yates, LLP, Attorneys and Counselors, Orange, California.

Thomas Nelson, Inc. titles may be purchased in bulk for educational, business, fund-raising, or sales promotional use. For information, please e-mail SpecialMarkets@ThomasNelson.com.

Library of Congress Cataloging-in-Publication

Walsh, Sheila.
    I'm not wonder woman : but God made me wonderful! / Sheila Walsh.
      p. cm.
    Includes bibliographical references.
    ISBN 978-0-7852-6293-0 (hardcover)
    ISBN 978-1-4002-0200-3 (trade paper)
    1. Christian women—Religious life. I. Title.
BV4527.W354 2006
248.8'43—dc22   2005030053

Printed in the United States of America
08 09 10 11 12 RRD 5 4 3 2 1

This book is dedicated with love and gratitude to Ruth Bell Graham. Ruth, you are beautiful inside and outside, and you have left an eternal imprint on my heart.

"Charm can fool you, and beauty can trick you, but a woman who respects the LORD should be praised."

— PROVERBS 31:30 (NCV)

Contents

The Woman Beneath the Cape

Wonder Woman 1: Monica the Magnificent
Here I come to save the day!

The alarm cut through the air like an amplified bugle call. Monica sat up in bed and reached for the appropriate button. The clock had delivered more than a simple wake-up call; it was the start of another mission. In her mind she could hear music. It sounded like a combination of the theme song to *Mission Impossible* and the "Hallelujah Chorus" from Handel's *Messiah*. Fully awake now, she bounded out of bed and headed for the shower. She was grateful that some companies had finally wised up and combined shampoo and conditioner in the same bottle, for she certainly didn't have time to do both. Her hair was cut in such a fashion that with a simple flip of the head it fell into a neat, shining bob. She sprayed her face with the new foundation in a can, applied a touch of blush and lip gloss, slipped into her suit, cape, and boots, and headed for the kitchen.

As she squeezed fresh orange juice and prepared bacon, eggs, and waffles for her husband and two children, she pressed *play* on the CD player above the stove and a warm, comforting voice began to read a passage from the Bible. At the end of the third Psalm, the voice moved to the New Testament and delivered the Sermon on the Mount with compassion and conviction. Two hymns later, it was time to wake the children.

Hannah and Peter bowed their heads and prayed before complimenting their mother on such a delicious and nutritious breakfast.

"Good morning, Light-of-my-life!" Simon said as he kissed his wife on the cheek. "What's on your schedule today?"

"Well, after I take the children to school," Monica said, "I'm meeting Gloria for coffee. She is having a few problems in her m-a-r-r-i-a-g-e. Then I volunteered to take lunch to two of the shut-ins in the church. After that, I'll collect the dry cleaning, shop for groceries, and pick up the children from school. I've invited your boss and his wife and three children over for supper."

"What a woman you are," Simon said, running his hands through Monica's clean, shining bob. "How do you do it all?"

Wonder Woman 2: Olivia the Overwhelmed
Does anyone know what day it is?

The alarm cut through the air like chalk on a dry board. Olivia reached over and pressed the snooze button of grace that gave her five more minutes. She pressed it one more time, then again until she became aware of the fact that her son was standing at the foot of the bed, yelling.

"Mom, we're late. That's two tardy slips this week!!"

She jumped out of bed, swirled some mouthwash around her gums, and pulled on the faded warm-up suit that was lying on the floor.

"Wake your sister!" she called after her son.

Olivia ran past her husband who was stretching out his bad back and headed for the kitchen. Grabbing two toaster pastries from an open box on the counter, she threw them into her purse and began the daily hunt for her car keys.

"Has anyone seen my keys?" she cried at the top of her lungs.

"The dog had them last night," her daughter said. "He hid them in the pizza box."

Olivia rummaged through the trash until she found her keys, well ensconced in a cold slice of pepperoni pizza.

"Kids, in the car—now!" she cried.

As she sped down the road, little pieces of cheese flew up from her key ring and stuck to her glasses.

"Kate, did you ever consider removing my keys from the pizza box before they had officially set?" she asked. But her daughter paid no attention, lost in the private world her MP3 player offered her each morning.

Olivia passed the cold pastries back to her children.

"We've missed chapel, Mom . . . again," her son said.

Cape and Boots or Crumpled Suit?

Do you identify with one of these women? Are you the kind of woman who has her routine down pat—you're organized, on top of things, a multitasker? Or are you more like Olivia, running behind time, hair barely combed, yelling at the kids to get in the car because you are late again?

I have been both women. I lived for several years in the cape-and-boots role, determined to show God and the world that no matter what the problem was, I was only a bugle call away. I have also been Olivia—when all I wanted to do was pull the covers over my head and pray that a bus would run over the bugle, and the world would go away and leave me alone. I used to be *Sheila the Magnificent*, and then I became *Sheila the Depressed* until God showed me the role that He had created for me, *Sheila the Wonderfully Made*.

Over the last ten years, I have traveled across America through the platform of an organization called *Women of Faith*. I have had the opportunity of speaking to over three million women. Each year we hold thirty conferences in arenas across the nation. Our theme changes each year—grace, hope, or faith—but the central message is the same: God sees you just as you are and loves you just as you are on crumpled suit days, and cape-and-boots days.

I have also had the pleasure of listening to many of the women that I meet at my book table and discovering that I am not alone in my quest to find out what on earth God had in mind when He created Eve, the very first woman.

Is There a Handbook Somewhere?

What exactly is expected of us as women? It doesn't seem to matter whether we are single, divorced, or married—most of us struggle to understand our divine purpose in life and to separate our dreams from the dreams others have for us, never mind adding in the huge spiritual pressure of what God might be looking for.

Perhaps you are familiar with these words found in the Old Testament: "'I say this because I know what I am planning for you,' says the LORD. 'I have good plans for you, not plans to hurt you. I will give you hope and a good future'" (Jer. 29:11 NCV).

This passage has brought comfort to many who love God, but I have often found it frustrating. On first read it's great to be assured that God knows the plans He has for us, but what if we miss them or spend so long trying to figure them out that we miss a good part of our lives? What if God's plans are not our plans, does that mean we have to be miserable to make God happy?

Did This Thing Come with Directions?

For his fortieth birthday, some friends gave my husband, Barry, a garden hammock. It came in five separate boxes and required some assembly. I am an assembly geek, so I told him that if he unpacked it,

I would assemble it. Unfortunately, Barry threw the instructions away with the rest of the trash, and I was left in the yard knee-deep in parts. My eight-year-old son, Christian, said that he would help. We tried for two hours to find which bits connected to other bits but to no avail. I sat on the grass, totally frustrated, when Barry called out enthusiastically, "All I can remember is that it said it was easy to assemble!"

I am deeply grateful that God is in control of this changing and confusing world. I firmly believe that God is good, and we can trust Him completely, but at times I have found myself wishing that He would let me see the plans He has; perhaps then the pieces of my life would make more sense. If I knew that what I was doing was on God's agenda for me, that it mattered to Him, it might be easier to embrace life, whether things were going well or going badly.

Warning Signs

Let me ask you a couple of questions: Do you think that it would be easier to cope with life's unexpected moments if you had advance warning of the storms ahead? Do you think that if you had a picture of how God was going to get you through them, you might not lose heart in the middle?

My immediate response to those two questions is to say *Yes!* But on reflection, I don't think I could cope with knowing everything that is to come. God promises grace for each situation as we go through it, not ahead of time.

Although the Monica and Olivia whom we just met are fictitious characters, I know many women who fall into one of those two types.

Secret Messages

I read somewhere that children are the best recorders of information and the poorest interpreters. I know that to be true in my own life. As I think back on my cape-and-boots days, I understand now that I determined as a child that I had better make myself useful to God and His people if I wanted to be loved and accepted. As children we take in everything around us, but we don't always interpret events correctly, which can lead us into a lifetime of choices based on incorrect information.

If you were sexually abused as a child, you might go on to a life of promiscuity, believing that this is the only way you can receive love.

If your parents divorced, you might assume that it was your fault and determine never to be any trouble to anyone again.

But what would it be like if we had been given a little advance notice of upcoming storms and a divine window through which to view them?

A Personal Letter from God

Imagine if each one of us was given a letter from God at birth. If we each had a road map of our life, how would that change the choices we make? If I had such a letter, mine might read a little like this:

Sheila, you have been placed in a very loving home. Enjoy your father as much as you can; don't miss a moment or a smile, for he will not be with you much longer. Capture his voice in your head and in your heart so that you will not forget. When he has come home to Me, I want you to know that this was not your fault, you did nothing to hurt him. This was his time. When he struck out in anger, it was not about you. His brain was wounded, and he didn't know what else to do. He is home now. He is safe. He loved you very much. You will live to do many of the things that he held in his heart. The sword that he laid down, you will pick up. Don't worry about your mom. I am her provider. She trusts in Me, and I will never fail her. At times she will need to cry alone, and as you grow older, you will understand that this mourning is a gift, a way to let go of some of the sorrow of this life. Remember, it doesn't matter what seems to be true or feels to be true, I am always with you, and I love you.

If you sat down today with a sheet of paper and wrote down the events that have shaped your life, how you see yourself, how you see others, how you misunderstood what happened to you at key moments, what would your letter look like? If you could sit down with yourself when you were five years old, what would you say, today, to that little girl, to help her make sense of her life and the events that have taken place or are just around the corner?

The reality is that none of us are given a letter from God telling us what lies ahead and how to respond. Some of us struggle for years to make sense of our lives and why we react the way we do. Some never even try.

Perhaps Monica the Magnificent understood as a child that the way to be loved is to be perfect. When she came home from school with good grades, her father smiled at her. When she was helpful in the kitchen or at school she would hear, "Monica, you are such a good girl." But there was a time when her grades slipped one term, and her father seemed removed and quiet, and her mother cried a lot. It wasn't long after that that her parents divorced and Monica knew, just knew, that it was her fault. She determined to never fail again. That vow was written in blood across her heart and soul. It colored all her choices. It wrote her script. If only there had been a piece of paper in her pocket that told her:

Monica, when your mom and dad divorce, it has nothing to do with you. They both love you just the way you are, good

grades and bad. They are broken people, Monica, who are try-
ing to find their way in a dark time. I am with you, and I am
with them. Hold on to My hand. You are a wonderful girl.

What about Olivia the Overwhelmed? Perhaps she grew up in a home where criticism was a daily reality. No matter how hard she tried, nothing was ever enough.

"Mom, Dad, I got an A-minus in math," she cried, excited to have upgraded her result from the previous term.

"Your brother got an A," was the disapproving response from her father.

As she began to develop as a young woman, there was no reassurance about her changing shape or hugs to tell her that puppy fat has a shelf life. She watched her mother despise her own reflection in the mirror and saw her future reflected there. Olivia got the message loud and clear that her life held little significance, so why try at all? If only that paper had been under her pillow each night:

Olivia, you are beautiful to Me. Your father's harsh words are
simply a recording of what he has heard his whole life. This is
the only song he knows. He loves you and often wishes he
knew a different tune. Your mother wants more for you than
she sees in herself, but she doesn't know how to give it to you.
You are full of possibility. You can do whatever you set your
heart on in My strength. Don't give up, Olivia. Don't give in.
I'm with you all the way.

Not a Letter but a Map

Not one of us had a letter like this to help us with the questions that we struggled with as we began to grow. But God did give us a map to help us navigate our lives. It's my prayer that in this book, through the Word of God and the stories of other women, we will be able to go right back to the very foundation stones of our lives and rebuild who we are based on what God has told us.

Remember the words of David the psalmist:

> For You formed my inward parts;
> You covered me in my mother's womb.
> I will praise You, for I am fearfully and wonderfully made;
> Marvelous are Your works,
> And *that* my soul knows very well.
> My frame was not hidden from You,
> When I was made in secret,
> *And* skillfully wrought in the lowest parts of the earth.
> Your eyes saw my substance, being yet unformed.
> And in Your book they all were written,
> The days fashioned for me,
> When *as yet there were* none of them. —Psalm 139:13–16 (NKJV)

I don't think that God calls any of us to be Wonder Woman, but He does want us to know that He has made us wonderful! Thank you for picking up this book. I trust that as we walk through the following chapters together, we will be able to identify where we have picked up wrong information and exchange that for the life of purpose and wonder that God calls us to. If you are worn-out from trying to get it all right, or if you have lost hope of ever getting anything right, my prayer for you is that God will give you a new vision and a new sense of purpose.

At the end of each chapter, there will be an invitation to a moment of reflection. I call it *A Look in the Mirror*. We live in such a fast-paced world that offers little opportunity to stop and breathe for a moment. Even reading books can turn into one more task on our to-do list. I want this book to impact where you are, right now. I don't want you to miss one thing that God might have for you.

Then there will be what I call *A Closet Prayer*. I use the imagery of a closet because that is the place where we often try to hide from God the things we are ashamed for Him to see. This prayer will be an opportunity to bring anything that has been uncovered by the Holy Spirit to your Father.

So let's have one big garage sale for all the capes and boots and begin!

Part One

Surprising Things You Might
Find in Wonder Woman's Closet

One

Insecurity:
I've got nothing to wear!

Are you tired? Worn out? Burned out on religion? Come to me.
Get away with me and you'll recover your life. I'll show you
how to take a real rest. Walk with me and work with me—
watch how I do it. Learn the unforced rhythms of grace. I
won't lay anything heavy or ill-fitting on you. Keep company
with me and you'll learn to live freely and lightly.

—MATTHEW 11:28–30 (THE MESSAGE)

I am woman, hear me roar!

—RAY BURTON AND HELEN REDDY, 1972

America is a couples' culture. If you are over the age of twenty-one and not married or heading in that direction, friends and family will attempt to fix you up with *Mr. Right*. If you are widowed or divorced, it is assumed that *Mr. Next* is just around the corner.

I didn't grow up in a culture like this. In Scotland, it is perfectly acceptable to be single. If you are widowed or divorced, it is more common to remain single than to remarry. That may be changing now as television presents a different picture, but when I was in my teens and twenties, a single person was viewed as a whole person rather than one in waiting or overlooked.

In church, we didn't have special groups or Bible studies for single people; they just had to muddle through like all the rest of us sinners. Perhaps our church leaders assumed that, rather than their needs being peculiar to them, single people had the same needs, hopes, and desires as those who were married—they just had more space in their beds.

When I first visited the United States in my early twenties, I became aware of how hard it was to be single in this country. The whole dating scene is a huge subculture, and, quite frankly, it's not something I ever excelled at!

An Early Engagement

Although I never dated much, I do have a past. I was engaged at ten! Not many people can claim that on a résumé. I didn't see it coming, so I was as surprised then as I'm sure you are now. There was a boy in my class at school whom I liked a lot. His name was Jim. I sat behind him and was fascinated by the way his dark hair curled on the collar of his school blazer. I had an overwhelming urge on a daily basis to touch his curly locks, but I was a good Baptist, so I suppressed my desire.

As Valentine's Day approached that year, I wondered if I dared send a card expressing my admiration for his brown eyes and his silken locks. My allowance did not provide for the kind of card that I wanted to give him, so I decided to make one. I took an empty Cornflakes box and cut it open to reveal the blank cardboard inside. I glued the rooster sides together so that I now had a clean slate on which to express myself.

There is something so full of possibility about a blank piece of paper. Before I committed to the first stroke of the paintbrush or the first word, it was perfect, full of promise, but sadly for me it was all downhill from that point on. In my head, I saw great beauty, but it never made it out onto the paper. So I remained the only one who knew of my potential to become a master painter or recipient of the Nobel Prize in Literature. All I can honestly say for that occasion is I did my best.

The following day was February the fourteenth, so I tucked the card inside my school bag. It was a cold, rainy day, as would be the norm between September and June of any given year on the west coast of Scotland. I crept into the classroom before the school bell rang and slipped the now-sodden card into Jim's desk. As my classmates began to file in, my heart was thumping in my chest. I panicked and considered removing the card before he saw it, but it was too late. I was sure he would laugh at me. I thought of all the extravagant, expensive cards that I had pored over in the drugstore. Some were so thickly padded they looked as if they had been made by a mattress company. My offering was pathetic. When the teacher asked us to open our desks and take out our workbooks, I almost fainted. Jim opened his desk, took out his book, and closed it again. *How could he have missed my soggy card?* Perhaps he saw it and was being kind enough to ignore it?

All day he said nothing. When the school bell rang at four o'clock, I headed home with a heavy heart. The following day, Jim approached me in the school yard before first bell and handed me a small package. I opened it, and inside was an engagement ring. It wasn't a toy or a cheap imitation; it was a gold band with three sapphires and two diamonds.

As you can imagine, I was shocked. I had no idea that one card could unlock such a floodgate. I asked him where he got it, and he informed me that he had found it on the beach one day and had been saving it for the right girl and the right moment.

He was not a man of many words; he simply looked at me and said, "This is it!"

My mother didn't see it that way, and that evening I had to take the ring to the police station and turn it in as lost property. After six months, the ring was unclaimed and returned to me so that my engagement period could continue. We smiled at each other at least twice a day, he put my name on his soccer ball, and I wrote his name inside my school bag in permanent ink, and that was the extent of our engagement.

Scottish teenagers didn't date much when I was growing up, but I dated less than most. I was fairly shy and uncomfortable with the woman I saw in the mirror. I saw myself as chubby and awkward. I have always been a klutz and have fallen down more stairs than Scarlett O'Hara was ever carried up.

Our school uniform was a white blouse with a navy and gold tie, grey skirt, navy blazer, and white socks. Other girls had pretty, feminine legs, but mine were a mass of bruises, cuts, and scrapes. Money was tight in our family, as Mom was raising three children by herself, so whenever I had my hair cut, she wanted her money's worth. My bangs were cut so short it took about a month before I looked human again. I'm surprised that I didn't pass away from brain freeze as I waited for the school bus on cold Scottish mornings!

All in all, I was not an inspiring sight. I didn't have a dad to tell me that he thought I looked beautiful, and I heard other voices that told me a different story.

Not So Wonderful

When I was sixteen years old, I was given the female lead of Maria in our school play, *West Side Story*. Before opening night, the whole school was invited to see us at dress rehearsal. I was nervous but excited too. It went well for a while until I took the stage with a mirror and began to sing, "I feel pretty, oh so pretty . . ."

Halfway through the first chorus, a boy stood up and screamed out, "Well, you sure don't look it!"

Laughter rippled through the high school auditorium. I was so embarrassed and hurt. I pressed on through the song, but my heart was breaking. I felt like such a fool. I made jokes about it afterwards with my friend, Moira, but that night I cried quietly into my pillow once my sister was asleep. It was one more voice confirming what I already knew: I was not one of the pretty ones.

The Standard Is Raised Even Higher

I fell in love once at college, but we parted before graduation. I decided to simply concentrate on serving God and live on the memories of a previous engagement, knowing that I could always say, sadly staring off into the distance, "I was engaged once . . ." Occasionally, I would have dinner with someone, but it never came to much. There is one date, however, that stands alone, redefining how inadequate I felt as a woman.

You Dated Who?

I was working for Youth for Christ at the time and was singing that weekend at a local Christian music festival. Most of us raised our own support, so there was no money for fancy outfits or jewelry. At the end of my set, a man introduced himself to me. He told me that he was with the record company that I had just recorded my first project with and asked if I would like to have dinner with him some time. I politely declined, but our paths crossed again a few weeks later, and after we talked for a while, I thought it might be fun. He showed up in a very flashy car and took me to a beautiful restaurant. During dinner, he asked me if I dated much.

"Not really," I said. "I'm very busy with my music and work. What about you?"

"I date a lot," he said. "My last date was very beautiful, beautiful and very successful."

"Well, how nice for you," I said. "Will you be seeing her again?"

"She had to return to America to continue filming her TV show," he replied nonchalantly.

"Wow! A TV star, would I know her?" I asked.

"It's Wonder Woman," he confided with great delight. "I dated Wonder Woman."

I stared at him for a moment not sure whether to laugh, applaud, or offer to pay for dinner. "You dated Wonder Woman? You dated *the* Wonder Woman, the one with the cape and the boots and the headband!?" I asked in disbelief.

"That's the one!" he said, trying unsuccessfully to look modest.

That evening I found myself staring in my bathroom mirror for a long time, taking inventory. I was twenty-three years old. *I have nice eyes and a good nose,* I told myself. *I could definitely stand to lose fifteen pounds. My hair is not so much styled as just . . . clean and dry.*

I looked over my meager wardrobe, but search as I did, there was not a cape in sight. I picked up a magazine that was lying on the floor beside my bed and flipped through the pages. The images I saw confirmed what I already knew: Wonder Woman I was not!

Ever Been There?

Have there been moments in your life when you suddenly saw yourself through someone else's eyes and the image was a disappointing one? Do you compare yourself to others and come up painfully short?

We live in a culture that is constantly redefining what physical beauty is, and even as Christian women, it is easy to fall into the trap of attempting to conform to that image.

In *Every Woman in the Bible*, Sue and Larry Richards write, "In the 1950s, beauty contest winners tended to be about 5'6" or 5'7" and weigh 140 to 150 pounds. Today's beauty contest winners are taller and generally 30 to 40 pounds lighter! Yet, today in the United States, women tend to be heavier than in the '50s and no taller!"[1]

Just as the gap between reality and society's ideal of female beauty widens, so does the gap between reality and the other expectations society and even the church place on women.[2] I believe that we have lost sight of the wonder of God's plan and vision for our lives.

It is my heart's cry to restore the marvelous picture of God's purpose for a woman's life. We should accept no less! It doesn't matter if you are fat or thin, tall or short, black or white, married or single— if we will exchange our view of our life for God's, it will transform the way we live.

But where do we start? Surely we need to go back to that first moment when a woman opened her eyes on planet Earth and felt pure joy coursing through her veins.

Before we try to imagine what that must have been like, let's take a moment and identify the places of humiliation and second-guessing in your life. You may find it helpful to write your responses in a journal. I have often been surprised by what I write when I am being very honest with myself. It can be therapeutic to put what we hide in our inner closet on paper.

A Look in the Mirror

Have you ever had a Maria moment? What was it?

How did that make you feel?

Do you compare yourself to other woman?

How do you honestly believe God sees you?

A Closet Prayer

This is a suggested prayer. Feel free to pray along with me or use your own words to express your heart to God.

Father God,

I confess that I don't always like what I see in my mirror. I compare myself to other women, and I don't feel as if I am enough. Help me to see that in You, I am more than enough.

Amen.

Two

Low Self-Esteem:
I don't like what I see in the mirror

> The LORD God made clothes from animal skins
> for the man and his wife and dressed them.
>
> —GENESIS 3:21 (NCV)

> *Mirror, mirror on the wall,*
> *Who is the fairest of them all?*
>
> —THE GRIMM BROTHERS, *SNOW WHITE*

She moved an arm, just a little. Feeling the ground beside her, she let dust run through her long, perfect fingers. As she moved, she heard a sound, a voice; she was not alone. The voice was beautiful. It made her laugh and cry at the same time. Slowly, Eve opened her eyes. It was bright, so bright that she closed them again for a moment. The voice spoke again. When she opened her eyes for a second time, she saw a hand stretched out to her. She reached toward the hand and was lifted off the ground until she stood erect in the sunshine.

Her hair tumbled down her back like cords of silk. They walked for just a little while, hand in hand. She couldn't see the face as it was so bright, but pure joy filled her heart and soul. When they stopped, she found herself looking into the eyes of a stranger. The bright one took her hand and placed it in the hand of the figure in front of her. He stared at her as tears began to run down his face. He took both of her hands in his and held them to his face as she began to sing. It was love, pure unadulterated love.

> And the man said,
> "Now, this is someone whose bones came from my bones,
>   whose body came from my body.
> I will call her 'woman,'
>   because she was taken out of man." —Genesis 2:23 (NCV)

I can only imagine how beautiful Eve must have been. She was God's perfect creation, made in His image. In the original Hebrew text, the two words *image (selem)* and *likeness (demut)* are linked together by a hyphen: *image-likeness*. What a statement!

Stop and think about that for a moment. God gave us the amazing gift of being made in his *image-likeness*. Through the years, artists and poets have tried to capture a picture of what Eve must have looked like. The blind poet John Milton wrote, "So absolute she seems and in herself complete." What a thought—*complete*. So in union with God and with her husband that she lacked nothing, absolutely nothing. Again Milton wrote, "O fairest of creation, last and best."[1]

George Herbert, the sixteenth-century Welsh poet, wrote of Eve, "The man was dust refined but the woman dust double-refined."[2] God made Adam from the dust of the ground, but after He had breathed life into Adam's nostrils and set him ablaze with joy and spirit, God made Eve. Just as we are born-again, as we rest under the blood that flowed from the wounded side of Christ, so Eve was born from the wound in Adam's side.

There would be no pain for Adam because there was as yet no sin in the world. God caused him to fall asleep, and as he slept, God worked. (My son and I joke that Barry is the next Adam because he's always sleeping as God works!)

Apart from her beauty, there were many things that marked Eve out as unique. She was never a baby or a teenager. She was never a daughter or a sister. She was never embarrassed, afraid, critical, insecure, misunderstood, or ashamed until that tragic moment when she chose to listen to a voice other than the voice of God. Listening to that voice and being seduced by its promise changed everything; it even changed her name.

Three Names

There are three names given to Adam's wife. First, God called them both *Adam.* "Male and female created he them; and blessed them, and called their name Adam, in the day when they were created" (Gen. 5:2 KJV).

God's design for men and women was not that we simply would have an association with each other or spar over the kitchen counter but that there would be an indissoluble unity between us—a communion that reflected the Godhead. How far we have fallen from that perfect place where there was only breath between us, no words to divide or punish, just love.

Adam originally called his wife "woman" because she was literally taken out of him, formed from one of his own ribs. But after they had eaten from the only tree that God told them never to touch, Adam called her *Eve.* His renaming of his wife was very significant. *Eve* means "mother of all living" or "life-giving." In Old

Testament times, a name was tremendously important. It told your story, prophetically declared who you were going to be, your character, your gifts, your future. Why then did Adam choose *Eve*, a name whose meaning was so positive? After all, didn't she offer him a piece of fruit from the forbidden tree and cost him everything?

He could have chosen a name that meant "bitterness," "shame," or even "death," but instead Adam chose the name *Eve*. He could not have understood the full prophetic nature of this name. They were about to be banished and God would reveal to Satan, in their presence, the redemption He would offer through Eve's seed. They just had no idea how long it would take or what it would cost the Father.

Two Trees

There were no shadows in Eden. There was no fear or threat, nothing but joy and laughter and love. God gave Adam the world. He brought every animal and bird to him and let him choose their names. Adam and Eve were allowed to eat the fruit of the tree of life so they would never die; the only fruit forbidden to them was from the tree that offered knowledge of good and evil.

As they had never sinned, they had no idea what they were about to do or what it would cost us all. They hadn't tasted the loneliness that hides in the darkness. We look back on that moment and think, *How could you have done that? How could you have exchanged a world of perfect peace and harmony for the world we live in now? How could you have been the very ones to introduce sin to the roots of your own family tree so that your firstborn son, the very first human baby, would become a murderer and take the life of your second son?*

What Have We Done?

But they didn't know. How could they have known what that one act of disobedience would cost? They had never tasted sin. George Matheson, the great Scottish theologian and hymn writer, said of Eve, "The temptation was not in itself the wish to transgress, but the will to possess."[3]

If Satan had approached Eve and told her to steal from the tree, I don't think she would have taken the fruit. He didn't say "steal," he said . . . "imagine." The very sin that had cost Lucifer his place as an angel of light, he now offered to this son and daughter of God. Lucifer had wanted power and was willing to risk everything to grasp it. His greed had cost him everything, and now his passion was to destroy all that God loved.

Our Moments in the Garden

Think about your own life. Think of the things that you have been drawn into that you later regret. Very rarely are they packaged as open rebellion. If you have ever been tempted to lie, I doubt Satan approached you with a complete unveiling of its consequences. *You don't have to tell the whole truth about yourself. Just lie—you'll get away with it. It will, however, come back to haunt you, and one lie will lead to another until you find yourself in a tangle of deception, and you will feel far away from God.*

He never gives us that much information; he simply says, "Imagine."

If you have ever had an affair, I'm pretty sure that Satan never approached you with the truth; he approached with a promise of more. *Do you see that man over there, the one who is looking at you, the one with the smile and the soft look in his eyes? Why don't you answer the question in those eyes? It will last for a little while, and it will devastate your family. In the end, you will ultimately despise him and yourself, but it will feel good for a while. Go on!* That kind of direct assault would be easy to resist, so instead of that, he just drops the word—*imagine*!

A New Face in the Mirror

From the moment that Adam and Eve ate the fruit from the forbidden tree, everything changed. The fruit offered knowledge and once they had ingested it, they couldn't give it back. Now they *knew* that they were naked. They had been naked since their first breath, but they had no idea, no shame, and no need for a covering between themselves or between them and God. For the first moment on Earth, a woman doubted herself and pulled back a little. We have been doing it ever since.

They gathered leaves and put together some type of covering for themselves, and then they did something previously unimaginable: they tried to hide from God. "Where are you?" God asked Adam and Eve. "Where are you?"

Can you imagine how they must have felt? They had never tasted dread before, but now it crept up their spines and sickened them to the depth of their stomachs. They tried to hide among the trees in the Garden, but that provided little cover from almighty God. So they came out and stood in their wretched garments and, I imagine, could not look God in the face. Adam and Eve had no way of knowing that the very thing they did would touch you and me.

Eve could not have conceived as she bit into the fruit that day that she had set the stage for every woman on the planet. As she stood before God, ashamed of her own image, condemned by her own heart, with distance between her and the one she loved, the first domino fell. Her life of wonder came crashing down—now she knew that she was not enough. And in an effort to regain her pre-Fall status, she began putting on her cape and boots.

A Whispered Promise

I find the book of Genesis full of shadows of the coming Christ. God rejected the clothes that Eve made; the clothes that she hoped might cover her sin. Instead, God provided a covering for them just as He does for you and for me. We can never hide our sin from God. We can never get rid of it on our own. We come to our Father in the name of Jesus, wearing our pathetic rags, and He clothes us in the righteousness of Christ. Since that day we have tried to be good enough for God, for others, and we have always come up short, but we never stop trying to undo what was done so long ago.

I was Eve that day as I looked at my twenty-three-year-old self in a full-length mirror in a hotel room in London, England.

So Long Ago in the Garden

He asked me if I would have lunch with him when he was in London on his latest tour. I was very flattered as I was a huge Larry Norman fan. To the uninitiated, Larry is known as the father of Christian rock. He was the first songwriter to combine rock-and-roll music and Christian lyrics.

I first heard him when I was sixteen years old. My friend Andree and I had managed to persuade our pastor to take us camping at *Greenbelt*, England's only Christian music-and-arts festival. Several years later, I was a recording artist, and Larry had heard my album and offered to help. He thought that it needed to be remixed, and he also offered to sing a duet with me on one song.

We met at the restaurant in the hotel where he was staying. I was very nervous during lunch and kept sending green peas flying all over the place as I tried unsuccessfully to stab them with a fork. When we were finished with lunch, he stood me in front of a full-length mirror and asked me this question, "Does that look like a star to you?" That was one of the easiest questions I'd ever been asked in my life—No!

In hindsight, I imagine he was trying to encourage me to dress better on stage or do something with my hair more than just washing it, but I heard far more. As I traveled home on the train that day, all that rang in my head was that I was a disappointment in person. Someone might listen to a song on the radio and like it, but if they actually met me, it would be a big letdown.

I had no desire to be a *star*. I wanted to communicate the love of God to those who didn't know Him, but the message I took home with me was that it didn't matter whether you were a Christian artist or a secular star, it was expected that you look better than I did. I couldn't change how I felt about myself inside, so I began the punishing pursuit of trying to change the outside.

For the next two years, I got into the terrible habit of running up debt on credit cards. I thought a new outfit would disguise what was wrong on the inside. I changed my hairstyle, my hair color, but it never felt like it was enough.

This is a merciless way to live because it will never be enough, and it doesn't work anyway. Part of the legacy of Eden demands that, as women, we will struggle with what we see reflected back at us. We have three things we can do with that: (1) we can bring how we feel about ourselves to God and ask Him to help us; (2) we can blame how we feel on what we are wearing and get something new;

(3) we can do what Adam and Eve did: we can shift the blame to someone else, and so begin the blame game that is a thin disguise for a heavy overcoat of shame. It is only with God's help that we can face all that is true about our lives.

A Look in the Mirror

Can you identify ways that Satan subtly tempts you?

What do you use to cover yourself when you feel ashamed?

What do you think was Eve's greatest loss?

A Closet Prayer

Father God,

I confess that at times I have been tempted and fallen into sin. I have tried to cover myself, but I confess that my only true covering is the blood of Your Son, Jesus. When I look in the mirror, help me to see what You see.

In Jesus' name,

Amen.

Three

An Overcoat of Shame:
I will never be good enough

The man said, "You gave this woman to me and she gave me
  fruit from the tree, so I ate it."
Then the LORD God said to the woman, "How could you have
  done such a thing?"
She answered, "The snake tricked me, so I ate the fruit."
—GENESIS 3:12–13 (NCV)

Take this overcoat of shame
it never did belong to me.
—ANNIE LENNOX, "THE GIFT" (DIVA), 1992

When I was a teenager, I had the most peculiar reaction when the telephone rang. For some reason, my heart would sink, and I would wonder what I had done wrong. It was a completely irrational response.
There was no deep, dark secret that I was waiting for someone to find
out. I wasn't a shoplifter or someone who cheated on tests at school.
I had no covert life of crime or sin, but the response was there.

If I were ever called to the headmaster's office at school, my heart
would be thumping as I made my way along the corridor, racking my
brain to think what I could have done to warrant such a summons.

The fear never matched reality. The headmaster usually either wanted to congratulate me for first place in a vocal competition representing our school or to ask me to be a school prefect. (A *prefect* in Scotland was an honor offered to senior students who had excelled in their schoolwork and were then given special privileges and a private sitting room.)

It would take years for me to begin to understand that I was wearing a heavy overcoat of shame that covered my heart and soul. Shame is part of the legacy of Eden that brings with it a sense of dread.

Shame or Guilt?

Shame is a different experience than guilt. Guilt tells me that I've *done* something wrong, but shame tells me that I *am* something wrong. I have encountered this in thousands of others—men, women, and children. Several years ago, I was invited to speak at a large church in Southern California. I spoke about the month I spent in a psychiatric institution, wrestling in the dark pit of clinical depression. I described my time there as a gift from God that finally helped me to see that for so long, I had been living as Wonder Woman. I had existed on the punishing treadmill of trying to be good enough for years, and when I finally fell to earth, it was actually a relief. I discovered that my internal closet was full of shame and anger, of fear and sadness that I had carried around since I was a child.

At the end of the service, I stayed around for a while to be available to anyone who wanted to talk. I was particularly struck by a very elegant woman who must have been in her late fifties. She told me that she was the CEO of a large successful computer software company. She had achieved all of her goals and more, but she said, "Inside I am miserable. When I was a little girl, my mother told me that I was a mistake. I carry that with me to this day. I am a mistake."

My heart ached for this woman who, to all outward appearances, had fulfilled her dreams but, inside, was still a wounded little girl who knew that she wasn't wanted. It didn't matter what she had *done*, she despised who she *was*. I understand that. Perhaps you do too.

She didn't have a letter from God telling her that she was loved and valued just for who she is. She didn't understand that with God there is no such thing as a mistake. I saw the loneliness in her eyes, for shame often keeps us isolated and lonely. It can make us pull away from others or attack them before they reject us. Blame often is shame veiled in a thin disguise.

It's Not My Fault!

The man said, "You gave this woman to me and she gave me fruit from the tree, so I ate it" (Gen. 3:12 NCV). From an experience of perfect harmony, Adam and Eve now found themselves in a cesspool of shifting the responsibility for what had taken place, even trying to lay it at the feet of God. "You gave this woman to me!" Adam's audacity knew no bounds. He inferred that everything was fine until God created Eve and brought her to him. And the blame game began. Adam blamed God and the woman; Eve blamed the snake— but God would hold each one of them accountable.

How quickly they fell from the wonder of their love for one another to this place of disassociation and distrust. There was barely a breath between them before, but now there was a huge chasm.

God first dealt with the one that had initiated the plan, the serpent. An approachable cover for Satan, the serpent had another form before the Fall. It is only after the Fall that, as part of the curse, he began to crawl on the ground. Within the short piece of poetry that God directs at Satan, there is the tragedy of our life here on earth and the promise of our deliverance:

The LORD God said to the snake,
"Because you did this,
    a curse will be put on you.
    You will be cursed as no other animal, tame or wild, will
    ever be.
You will crawl on your stomach,
    and you will eat dust all the days of your life.
I will make you and the woman
    enemies to each other.
Your descendants and her descendants
    will be enemies.
One of her descendants will crush your head,
    and you will bite his heel." —Genesis 3:14–15 (NCV)

Genesis makes it clear that Satan will be our enemy all the days that we walk on this earth, but God has a plan. Even there in the Garden, in the place of bitter betrayal and shame, God reveals that from the very woman whom Satan took captive will come One who will ultimately crush him.

This will not be without a price. The price will be shared by every man, woman, and child who lives, but the ultimate price will be paid for by Christ, the Son of God, who will allow Satan to bruise His heel on Calvary so that you and I will be free at last.

The Curse for Eve

God turns next to Eve.

Then God said to the woman,
"I will cause you to have much trouble
  when you are pregnant,

> and when you give birth to children,
>   you will have great pain.
> You will greatly desire your husband,
>   but he will rule over you." —Genesis 3:16 (NCV)

There is not a woman who has ever given birth that cannot say a loud *Amen* to that! It's clear that childbirth was never meant to include pain, but that is part of what we carry as daughters of Eve. Even there in the physical reality of giving birth, we see the joining together of the inheritance of Eden and the free gift of God in Christ. The pain that we experience in giving birth is the result of our sin, but the gift of life, in a child, is the promise of God. Even in God's judgment of us, there is always mercy, always hope, promise, and a future.

When I consulted my study Bibles and commentaries, I discovered most theologians agree that the text, "You will greatly desire your husband, but he will rule over you" was the beginning of the great battle of the sexes. The word *desire* can also be translated as "an attempt to control or take over."

"We can paraphrase the last two lines of this verse this way: 'You will now have a tendency to dominate your husband, and he will have the tendency to act as a tyrant over you.'" [1]

How many of us can relate to that! Whether it's trying to give directions while our husbands are driving or taking the initiative in spiritual matters, many of us struggle with a compulsion to overwhelm our husbands, which, in turn, challenges them to reassert their independence.

Adam's Lot

God's words to Adam are solemn and contain the seed of every man's struggle.

Then God said to the man, "You listened to what your wife said, and you ate fruit from the tree from which I commanded you not to eat.

"So I will put a curse on the ground,
   and you will have to work very hard for your food.
In pain you will eat its food
   all the days of your life.
The ground will produce thorns and weeds for you,
   and you will eat the plants of the field.
You will sweat and work hard for your food.
Later you will return to the ground,
   because you were taken from it.
You are dust,
   and when you die, you will return to the dust."
   —Genesis 3:17–19

It seems clear that up until that point work was not a chore but a joy. There were no weeds to contend with in the Garden. The ground was easy to tend, but now everything would be difficult and frustrating. I don't know a man alive who has not tasted of this curse. It is the most primal instinct in every man to want to work hard and produce good results to take care of his family, but so often it is an uphill battle. Perhaps you have observed this with your dad or your husband or brothers. They put so much effort into what they do, only to meet with weeds and thistles instead of the expected fruit. To Adam, God declares that now, just as he came from dust, he must return to dust. Instead of living forever as God planned, Adam and his children and his children's children would taste death. Paul makes reference to this reality in his letter to the church in Rome: "Sin came into the world because of what one man did, and with sin came death. This is why everyone must die—because everyone sinned" (Rom. 5:12 NCV).

The Shame of Banishment

So Adam and Eve were made to leave the Garden and begin laboring in the very dust from which Adam was created. I have often wondered when Eve became pregnant with her firstborn, Cain, did she think this was the promised one who would crush the serpent's head? It would seem a natural conclusion. How could she know how many generations would pass before the birth of Christ? How could she know that this boy she carried, instead of becoming a deliverer, would become a murderer?

The Reality of Shame

Webster's Dictionary defines *shame* as "a painful emotion caused by consciousness of guilt, shortcoming, or impropriety." I did some research on *shame* on the Internet and discovered a few interesting offers. There is a Harvard-endorsed program that promises a proven, fast cure for shame. The Sedona Method offers freedom from self-recrimination in several easy steps. It suggests that letting go of shame is completely in our control. Just as dropping a pencil to the floor is our choice if it is in our hands so, too, with letting go of disturbing emotions such as shame.

I read some of the online testimonials, and the results suggested that if we would employ this method of letting go of negative emotions, we would be able to do anything from losing twenty pounds to becoming a millionaire! I am in no position to be able to judge what they are offering, but I do know that in my own life, no matter how many times or in how many ways I tried to get rid of shame, it found its way back to me until I brought it to the Cross and let Jesus deal with it. Shame knew my address, and it wasn't enough to drop it; I had to take it where it belonged.

Born Again, Again

I sat in the back row of a small church in Washington, D.C., and listened as the pastor spoke. He said, "Some of you feel as if you are dead inside. You can almost hear them begin to heap the dirt on top of your casket lid. But Jesus is here. All you have to do is stretch out one hand. He will reach in and pull you free."

I was on a morning pass from a psychiatric ward and was sitting beside the nurse who had accompanied me. As I listened to those words, I knew that God was talking to me. I was thirty-six years old and had given my life to Christ when I was eleven, but I had never given Him my shame.

For years, I had worn this punishing cape that told me there was something wrong with me, so I determined to make myself useful to God and others for the rest of my life. I donned the cape and boots and threw myself into doing everything and being everything a woman could be, but it was never enough.

As I sat there watching the sunlight stream through the stained-glass windows, I heard God offering to exchange my burden for the one He would give me. I knew He was telling me that if I would come to Him in my tattered cape, He would give me a new coat. I had never walked to the front of a church in response to a call in my whole life, but I ran to the front of the church that day and lay facedown in front of the altar. I told my Father that I was worn-out; I couldn't live this way anymore. I told Him that I was not Wonder Woman. *I have never felt more worthless or more loved.*

It was clear to me that I had nothing to bring to the table but my broken heart, and He accepted me just as I was. As that cape of shame fell off my shoulders that day, it seemed to me that I was born again once more. Even though I had walked with Christ for years, I had dragged my shame with me. But when I stood up, I was a different woman. For the first time, I understood clearly that I am a broken, flawed daughter of Eve but that God loves me as I am and has taken my shame from me.

If you have never struggled with shame, it is hard to describe what it is like to be set free from its sickening grip. It is one of God's greatest gifts to us this side of seeing Him face-to-face. I was to discover that I would have to keep giving it back to Him since shame has a homing device and loves to return to the place it used to rest. I realized that I would also need the help of a godly counselor to help me dig up all its roots.

In just a few short weeks after being released from the hospital, I began my drive across the country from Virginia on the East Coast to a new life in California on the West Coast. As I drove, I put my new Annie Lennox CD, *Diva,* in the car player and listened as she sang,

> Take this overcoat of shame
> it never did belong to me.

I didn't realize then how many other surprising items were still in my closet.

A Look in the Mirror

Can you identify places of shame in your own life?

Can you write down the areas where you feel as if you are something wrong instead of someone who has done something wrong?

Can you trace the roots of your shame?

A Closet Prayer

Father God,

I acknowledge before You that at times I feel overwhelmed by shame. I ask You to help me drop this overcoat at the Cross and put on the garment You have made for me. Just as You dressed Eve, I ask that You would dress me.

In Jesus' name,

Amen.

Four

Anger:

I'm losing control

When you are angry, do not sin.
 Think about these things quietly as you go to bed.

—PSALM 4:4 (NCV)

I was angry with my friend; I told my wrath, my wrath did end.
I was angry with my foe: I told it not, my wrath did grow.

—WILLIAM BLAKE (1757–1827), A POISON TREE

When I was fifteen years old, I played the part of Anger inside the mind of a man who was about to commit murder. It was a very avant-garde play, each character an emotion. My mother thought that *Little Women* would have been a better choice, but our hip new English teacher had moved beyond the classics.

I have no idea why she chose me to play Anger as I was a very mild-mannered teenager. She must have thought each one of us had a cauldron bubbling just below the surface. But as I learned my lines, I struggled to find my cauldron! By dress rehearsal our teacher was on the edge.

"Is that supposed to be anger? You're not mad enough to spank a hamster!"

"I'm trying," I said.

"Well try harder—where is your anger? Tap into the rage!"

"I don't have any—I'm a Baptist!"

Well, let me just say to that: Ha! Ha! Ha! I found out later in life that I had a lot of stuff going on under the surface of my neat, contained Christian life. Anger is something we don't talk about much in the church, which, in my experience, bears witness to the fact that it's a huge problem. The things that we don't talk about, such as depression, addiction to online pornography, sexual abuse, anger, and shame, are rife within our churches. Most pastors do not choose "Anger" as a sermon topic, but if they do, they usually focus on the passage from Ephesians—be angry and sin not. (Eph. 4:26) But how do we do that?

I have seen over the years that anger is often linked to fear and chained to rejection. We can see that reality with the very first family.

Anger and Rejection

Abel brought the best parts from some of the firstborn of his flock. The LORD accepted Abel and his gift, but he did not accept Cain and his gift. So Cain became very angry and felt rejected.

The LORD asked Cain, "Why are you angry? Why do you look so unhappy?"—Genesis 4:4–6 (NCV)

At first read, it's hard to understand why Abel's offering was accepted and Cain's was not. Cain worked the land, so it seems logical that he would offer produce of the land. Abel worked with the flocks, so he brought an offering from his flock. However, Abel's gift was from the firstborn lambs—he brought the very best he had to give—but Cain brought a token gift. God always looks beyond the gift to the state of our hearts. What God saw in Cain's heart was a careless gesture compared to the act of worship coming out of his brother's heart. There is also a more far-reaching meaning in that Abel brought a perfect, flawless lamb—a fore-shadowing of the coming Christ who would shed His innocent blood in our place. Cain brought the work of his hands, which was not acceptable just as our works have no merit for redemption. We can only come to the Father under the cover of the blood of the Lamb.

But can you see God's mercy in that He gave Cain another chance and a warning? "If you do things well, I will accept you, but if you do not do them well, sin is ready to attack you. Sin wants you, but you must rule over it" (Gen. 4:7 NCV).

Here is one of those crossroad moments. We all have them. We have a moment to choose which path we'll take. Satan can tempt us, but he can't push us onto a path. We choose that for ourselves, and once we do, should we choose the path of giving in to our unbridled emotions, he is right there waiting for us.

Cain had a moment to choose as his emotions bubbled under the surface. He was jealous that Abel's offering was accepted the first time and his was not. I'm sure there was defensiveness in his response, too, which is so often present when we know that we have done the wrong thing. That jealousy gave birth to rejection and fueled his anger, and Cain became forever known as the first murderer in human history.

Killing Me Softly

Cain's story may seem a world away from where you live, but the seed is there. There are many forms of murder. We can kill someone by cutting them out of our lives. Our very words can be lethal weapons, leaving deadly wounds in the heart and soul of someone else. I was surprised when I realized how much anger I had stuffed into the back of the closet of my heart.

Facing My Internal Demons

I cannot remember a time in my teenage years when I felt free to express anger. Anger was something that terrified me. My earliest experience with anger was from my father. After a massive hemorrhage in his brain, his anger was not a reasonable thing. It was no longer linked to a particular catalyst. It became an internal rage that he had no control over, and he would lash out at unpredictable moments and in ways that were very alarming to a child.

After his death, I equated anger with violence. As I moved through my teenage years and into my twenties, I learned to suppress what I felt. If I was angry about something, I just stuffed it in the back of the closet. If someone was unkind or cruel, I took it all in and crammed it back there in the dark. I had no skills for dealing with injustice or expressing strong emotion. I dreaded being out of control.

There were one or two moments when the rage broke through, but it was never in my own defense—only if someone I loved was being wronged. I once punched a girl in the face because she called my brother, Stephen, "Metal-legs" as he wore metal braces to correct his feet from turning in.

One of the first things my therapist did as I spent time in a psychiatric unit was to hold up a chart describing various emotions and ask me to identify the ones I was familiar with. I felt as if I were a Martian, and the language he spoke wasn't used on my planet. I honestly tried to identify with the words: *joy, peace, contentment, anger, fear.*

I began to realize that when you suppress one emotion, it's as if you anesthetize your whole heart. Anger is part of life. It's like fire, and when it's used properly, it can be very productive, but if misused it is deadly.

I have learned to take my anger first and foremost to God. No matter what I am angry about, I unload everything I am feeling before Him. Then I ask Him for the wisdom to pick up what would be helpful and productive and leave the stuff that is linked to my pride or hurt feelings with Him. I think of that as *clean* anger. Then I pray for the insight to express what I am feeling in an appropriate way.

When we do not acknowledge or deal with anger, it leaks out at unexpected moments.

Helpless

I saw it in my sweet son's eyes and in his actions. He felt helpless and out of control, and that had birthed anger in his five-year-old heart. He was very attached to his papa. William, my father-in-law, had lived with us for two years and was the kind of grandfather every boy should have. His patience was endless and his stories hilarious. But one night, William collapsed in his bathroom, suffering a massive heart attack. Christian and I were the only ones home with him. The EMS workers did all they could to revive him as the ambulance headed to our local hospital. Christian and I followed in our car. He was very quiet as we drove. When we arrived, a nurse took Christian to a separate room, and the doctor told me that William hadn't made it.

In the days and weeks that followed, I watched my son grieve, and I grieved with him. His tears flowed freely, and I was glad that he was able to express what he was feeling, but one day I saw a new emotion grab hold of him. As he walked past a chair where our cat, Lily, was sitting, he pushed her off. I had never seen him do something like that before. We went for a long walk by the golf course outside our home and, after a while, sat down on the grass to talk.

"Christian, are you feeling angry, baby?"

"Yes, Mommy," he said.

"Can you talk to me about it?"

"You told me that God answers our prayers. I prayed that God would let my papa live, and He didn't answer me. I don't understand."

Which one of us has not found ourselves in that place? One of the greatest struggles of the Christian life is wrestling with the knowledge that God is able to answer all our prayers as we ask them, and yet often He does not answer in the way we want Him to.

I received an e-mail from a woman asking me to pray for her son who was struggling with a very aggressive form of cancer. She told me that as a family, they were asking God to heal her son. Several months later, she wrote to tell me that he had died. She wrote, "We asked God to heal him, but now are not very happy with the way He did it."

Nothing has worked properly since the Garden of Eden. Even as I was writing this morning, a friend sent me an instant message online, and I heard in her words all the frustration and disappointment of life as we must live it now. Her son is in some trouble, and she feels helpless to do anything about it. She wrote, "I'm on a wild roller coaster that takes me through sadness, anger, helplessness, disappointment, frustration, and then drops me back to sadness and anger again."

Anger is a defense mechanism, and when we feel out of control, it is an easily accessible tool. It makes us feel as if we are *doing something*.

What I tried to help my son understand as he dealt with very valid feelings of anger is that when you push it under the surface, it will re-emerge somewhere down the line, at times in the most unfortunate circumstances.

A Series of Unfortunate Events

Moses was a man who walked closely with God. He was described in Deuteronomy as the greatest prophet of Israel. "Now Moses was very humble. He was the least proud person on earth" (Num. 12:3 NCV).

Although Moses was a man who lived humbly, a moment of anger changed his life forever. Even a man like Moses, described as "the least proud person on earth," had some things stuffed into the back of his closet that in an unguarded moment exploded and changed his destiny. Perhaps you remember there were two key moments in his life when anger burst through and impacted his destiny.

These Are My People

The first is recorded in Exodus chapter two. The king of Egypt was afraid that the Israelites were becoming too strong and too numerous, so he ordered that every Hebrew baby boy should be thrown into the Nile river. When Moses was born, his mother and sister came up with a plan to save his life. They put him in a basket and watched as it floated down the Nile to where the daughter of the king was bathing with her attendants. They heard the baby's cries, and when the king's daughter saw this tiny one, her heart went out to him.

Moses's sister was watching as this unfolded, and she approached and asked if she might find someone to breastfeed the baby until he was weaned, usually at about four years of age then. So Moses was given back to his mother until he was a little boy. Then she took him to the palace to be raised as the king's grandson.

I wonder what that must have done to a child. We read the story as part of history and might even imagine that it would be a privilege to be raised in a royal palace, but what about his feelings for his mother and his sister? Can you imagine a child of four being taken away from his mom and family to be raised by strangers who even spoke a different language?

He must have been told why he was being taken there. He must have known as he grew that the man he was to call Grandfather was responsible for the slaughter of the Hebrew boys and the reason why he had no male playmates his own age.

I'm sure his mom warned him to be wise and make the most of his life that had been rescued from the river. But one day, when Moses was about forty years old, he saw something that pushed him over the edge. He went to see how his people were being treated and saw that they were being pushed to work harder and harder. One man was being beaten mercilessly, and something inside Moses snapped. He killed the Egyptian responsible for the unreasonable punishment. His days in the palace were over, and he had to run for his life. As he ran, he took his deep childhood wounds with him.

A Moment of Anger that Cost the Promised Land

If you are familiar with the rest of the story, you will remember that God called Moses to return years later to the very palace he had run away from and ask Pharaoh to let God's people go. At this point, Moses was eighty years old. After God sent many harsh plagues against the Egyptian people, Pharaoh finally let them go.

Instead of being grateful and humbled by God's deliverance, the people constantly complained and rebelled. In an ultimate act of betrayal, as Moses was receiving God's law on Mount Sinai, they made a calf out of gold and bowed down to worship it. When God saw what they were doing, He told Moses to leave Him alone so that His anger could burn against the people and He could destroy them. Moses asked God to have mercy on them. He put himself between the wrath of God and the open rebellion of the Israelites. He reminded God of His promise to Abraham that his descendants would outnumber the stars.

So God changed His mind, but He made them wander in the wilderness for forty years until every one of their unbelieving generation had died. Only their sons and daughters were allowed to cross over into the Promised Land.

In their wanderings, they came to a place called Zin. They were thirsty, and they had no water, and, as usual, they complained bitterly to Moses. God told Moses to speak to a rock, and water would pour out of it. At this point, Moses was beyond being frustrated with the people. So instead of speaking to the rock, as God had commanded, he allowed the rage inside of him to take over, and he *struck* the rock twice with his staff.

For that act, God told him that he would not enter the Promised Land. That may seem a harsh judgment, but what Moses did has great theological and prophetic implications.

Christ the Rock

We find a clue in Paul's first letter to the Church in Corinth:

> Brothers and sisters, I want you to know what happened to our ancestors who followed Moses. They were all under the cloud and all went through the sea. They were all baptized as followers of Moses in the cloud and in the sea. They all ate the same spiritual food, and all drank the same spiritual drink. They drank from that spiritual rock that followed them, and that rock was Christ. —1 Corinthians 10:1–4 (NCV)

When the children of Israel were heading toward Mount Sinai, God told Moses to strike the rock once. He obeyed, and water poured out. This second time, the command was just to speak to the rock, and it would provide life-giving water. The rock represented Christ, and what He would do on the Cross. Hebrews 10:10 tells us:

"And because of this, we are made holy through the sacrifice Christ made in his body once and for all time" (NCV). Christ was struck once and for all time. When Moses let his rage explode, he distorted the typology of Christ's sacrifice, by striking twice and three times. God expected a lot of Moses because He revealed a lot of Himself to him. But even in this judgment, there was mercy. Moses was not allowed to cross over into the Promised Land, but he was allowed to stand on the mountainside and see across the Jordan River. When Moses died, we were given one of the most intimate pictures of our Father God; He was the one who buried Moses, His prophet and friend. "So Moses the servant of the LORD died there in the land of Moab, according to the word of the LORD. And He buried him in a valley in the land of Moab, opposite Beth Peor; but no one knows his grave to this day" (Deut. 34:5–6 NKJV).

Anger can serve us and serve God well. One thing is clear: anger, that is, the right kind of anger, is not a quick fuse that blows up in a moment and is out of control. James warns us about that kind of anger: "My dear brothers and sisters, always be willing to listen and slow to speak. Do not become angry easily, because anger will not help you live the right kind of life God wants" (James 1:19–20 NCV).

As my counselor encouraged me to consider why I had hidden anger in my heart for so long, I saw that lurking just under the surface was the real culprit—fear.

A Look in the Mirror

What are the issues that make you angry?

How do you handle anger when you feel it beginning to rise up?

What would be an appropriate way to express anger?

A Closet Prayer

Father God,

I confess to You that many times I have allowed anger to take over. At other times I have held it in, and it has grown. Help me to bring my anger to You for grace and mercy.

In Jesus' name,

Amen.

Five

Fear:

I'm afraid of what the future might hold

> Not seeing, still we know—
> Not knowing, guess—
> Not guessing, smile and hide
> And half caress—
>
> And quake—and turn away,
> Seraphic fear—
> Is Eden's innuendo
> "If you dare"?

—EMILY DICKINSON (1830–1867), POEM 1518

> I am frightened inside;
>   the terror of death has attacked me.
> I am scared and shaking,
>   and terror grips me.
> I said, "I wish I had wings like a dove.
>   Then I would fly away and rest.
> I would wander far away
>   and stay in the desert.
> I would hurry to my place of escape,
>   far away from the wind and storm."
>
>   —PSALM 55:4–8 (NCV)

"It starts in five minutes," my sister would announce as Mom and I prepared the late-night snacks. Every Friday night was a trip down terror avenue in the Walsh household. The series was called *Don't Watch Alone*! Each week it would be a different movie from the old black-and-white horror classics such as *Frankenstein* or *The Wolf Man*.

I was seventeen, and my sister, Frances, was nineteen. My brother was safely tucked in bed upstairs, oblivious to the spine-tingling tales the rest of us dared to watch. Mom would sit in her favorite chair by the fire, Frances occupied the other, and I sat on the floor, watching the movie through a hole in my teddy bear's stomach. (He was a very brave bear!)

Each week, Mom would say, "I don't think you should watch this week, Sheila. You were scared last week."

"No, I was just kidding," I would reply.

"Well, let me make it clear, I am not singing through the entire hymn book before we go to sleep again," Frances would add.

"Of course not," I would say. "Anyway, we just sang two hymns!"

The music would start, and it was creepy. It was the music that always got me. If we had turned the volume off, I would have been fine, but Frances seemed reluctant to do that. I could tell when the scary bits were coming by the crescendo in the music, and I would bury my face in Big Billy's tummy, occasionally peeking out through the hole. Finally, the bad beast would be taken care of and all Frances wanted to do was sleep, but I would plead, "Just one verse of 'Abide with Me.' Please! Then a quick chorus of 'Victory in Jesus,' and I'll be fine."

It is one thing to watch a silly movie, then turn it off and be fine after a few reassuring bars of what is true, but it is quite another when it seems as if the dark music and scary stranger live in the basement of your soul. Fear takes all sorts of shapes.

It can manifest itself in the unknown world of the *what-ifs*. It can be based on a difficult memory from your past that left a scar. It can be rooted in a dread of being out of control.

The What-Ifs

There is nothing more powerful to conjure up terrible possibilities than our own imaginations. I find myself thinking about things now that I would not have imagined a few years ago.

We live in Dallas, Texas, which is a bigger city than our old home of Nashville, Tennessee, and seems to carry the potential of more frightening possibilities. Every time there is an Amber Alert for a missing child, my heart freezes. I don't know whether these things happen more often now or if it's just that we hear about them more through TV, radio, and the Internet. In 2005, two children were kidnapped from their backyards just a few miles from where we live; both children were found dead. It is every parent's worst nightmare. Yet I know that it would be worse to have your child missing and never know what happened to them.

When I see pictures of missing children who have been gone for two or three years, I often wonder what has happened to their families during the weeks and months that they have waited and imagined. I stop and pray that they will know the presence of the Lord, for without the hope that there is an eternity free from pain and fear, how could they survive?

Each day, as I drop Christian off at school, we pray together. I pray for his protection and for the protection of every child in the school. We have strict security rules as a family. Christian knows to never accompany a stranger or even a friend unless they know our password. We do all we know to do, believing also in the sovereignty of our God. I know that before Christian was born, every day of his life was recorded in God's book. I believe that nothing will happen to him that hasn't passed through the merciful hands of our Father, but at times I still catch myself dwelling on images that terrify me—the *what-ifs* are always with us. All we can do is drag our will in line with the will of God and remind ourselves that we are promised grace for this day. Whatever happens to us, God will be with us. "Do not worry about anything, but pray and ask God for everything you need, always giving thanks. And God's peace, which is so great we cannot understand it, will keep your hearts and minds in Christ Jesus" (Phil. 4:6–7 NCV).

I know that prayer and peace are God's gifts to us in this world; it's just hard to stay there sometimes. The *what-ifs* began in Eden and have plagued us ever since. Sometimes they are based on our fear of being found out, caught in our sin.

Caught

Adam feared, *What if God finds out what we did?* "I heard Your voice in the garden, and I was afraid" (Gen. 3:10 NKJV). What if He is angry with us?

We can trace that thread through the lives of those who came after Adam. We see it in Jacob who wanted to fool his father into thinking that he was actually his brother, Esau. "If my father touches me, he will know I am not Esau. Then he will not bless me but will place a curse on me because I tried to trick him" (Gen. 27:12 NCV).

We see it again in the story of Joseph, which is found in Genesis 37. His brothers sold him into slavery hoping to get rid of him once and for all, but when they saw him again, he had become a very powerful man. "What if Joseph is still angry with us? We did many wrong things to him. What if he plans to pay us back?" (Gen. 50:15 NCV).

I know that dread, the fear that is brought on by your own sin.

When I was about ten years old, I took some money from my mom's wallet. It was the equivalent of about one dollar. I didn't think she would miss it, so when she asked my brother, sister, and me at dinner if any of us had taken money from her purse, I was horrified. I compounded my initial sin by lying. Now I was in deep! All that evening my heart was pounding in my chest. I felt—*separate*. My sin had put a wall between me and my mother. Now the fear of the *what-ifs* kicked in. *What if I'm found out? What if she is so disappointed in me? What if my mom doesn't love me anymore?*

I couldn't sleep that night so I got up and told my mom that not only had I taken the money but I had also lied about it. Even though I was disciplined for stealing and lying, I was still relieved to be free of the isolation of my sin.

Not Enough

Sometimes the *what-ifs* stem from a fear that we can't do what someone is asking us to do. In our insecurity, we believe that we don't have what it takes. Moses felt that way when God called him to be His mouthpiece. Moses answered, "What if the people of Israel do not believe me or listen to me? What if they say, 'The LORD did not appear to you'?" (Ex. 4:1 NCV).

Has anyone ever asked you to do something, and suddenly, you were overwhelmed by fear? It may even have been an opportunity that you had prayed for, but when the moment came, self-doubt and fear came rushing in.

My first public speech was enough of a trauma to put an end to any aspiring speaker's career! I was about twelve, I think, and one of our Sunday school teachers was getting married. She had served as a teacher for years and was much loved. The church bought a beautiful tea service for her, and I was to make the speech as we presented the gift to her. I would talk about Elizabeth's years of service and how much we all loved her and what a blessed man her fiancé was. I rehearsed and rehearsed until my family was sick of hearing me. I even practiced in front of my mom's full-length mirror, so I could check my posture.

Then came the big night. When my moment came, I walked onto the stage, paused to collect myself, and then looked out at the crowd and . . . froze. I stood for what seemed like three hours and twenty-five minutes but was probably about thirty seconds. My mom and sister tried to feed me lines from their vantage point on the front row, but I couldn't hear anything, just the crushing sound of my silence. Finally, I blurted out, "When we heard that you were getting married, we were really surprised!"

I thrust the tea service at her and ran off stage into the ladies bathroom and stayed there until I graduated from college!

Obviously, I recovered as public speaking is now a huge part of my life, but it was years before I was able to overcome the kind of fear that interfered with what I am called to do. I'm often asked by other women, who find themselves in the same terrified place that I was, how I was able to get over the kind of fear that is paralyzing. Relief came for me in a very simple story that I'm sure is familiar to you, a story about a young boy and his lunch. In Sunday school, it's called "the loaves and the fishes." As I studied that miracle, I began to see things that I had never seen before.

The Packed Lunch

Jesus was teaching the crowd that had followed Him, and He saw that they were hungry, so He asked His disciples where they could buy enough food to feed everyone. The men told Jesus that they would need to work for a month to feed the crowd before them. The disciple Andrew brought all he could find, which was a boy's lunch of five barley loaves and two small fish. Jesus took the food, blessed it, broke it, and gave it to the disciples to feed the crowd. There was more than enough.

When the event was over, do you think the boy said to his mother, "I can't believe what I did today. I fed thousands of people, not one person was left hungry—I'm amazing!" It's my guess that the boy was amazed by what Jesus did and was never the same again.

That is how I feel every time I get up on a platform with my barley loaves and fish; I can't wait to see what Jesus will do this time. That's all we are asked to do. We are asked to show up with whatever God has packed for us that day and trust that it will be enough. Our Father sends us off into each day with just what we will need for everything we will encounter in that day. As a day unfolds, the events may surprise us, but they do not surprise Him. When you find yourself in a hospital waiting room, when your husband walks out on you, when you lose your job, when you stand on a platform to tell your story, when you are facing the unthinkable—no matter what—offer what little faith and courage you have to your Father, and He will make it enough.

This Is Not Imagination, It Is Real

Fear can also be born out of a very real experience that has left its mark on us. When Barry, my husband, was a little boy, his days were marked by fear. His godmother died of cancer, and having tasted the death of someone so close, Barry now transferred that fear onto losing his father. Every day, when it would be time for his dad to come home from work, Barry would stand out in the driveway with tears running down his face. If his dad was even five minutes late for some reason, Barry would just know that something terrible had happened to him. It took many years for Barry to be able, with God's help, to change the way he responded to irrational fear.

When we were first married, I bought an ornament for our tree that said, *Our First Christmas.* When we began to decorate our tree, I dropped it and it smashed. Barry looked stricken and asked me what I thought it meant. I told him that it meant he had married a klutz—nothing more!

I have talked with many women, in second marriages because of infidelity committed by their first spouse, who are terrified that this new husband will be unfaithful too. The past experiences of betrayal have followed them into their new lives, and they are unable to enjoy what God has given them for fear that history will repeat itself. Fear can be a brick wall between people.

One lady told me that she had destroyed her second marriage because of the way she badgered her husband and followed him, all born out of the fear that he would do what her first husband did. Through bitter tears, she told me that she knew he was a good man, but she could not control her fear, and it had cost her dearly.

Out of Control

Fear can also come from feeling helpless. No Wonder Woman wants to admit this, but often, just lurking under the cape, is a terror of losing control, and that fear drives us to try and grasp control wherever we can.

When this book is published in 2006, I will turn fifty! I still can hardly believe that. In my mind, my mom is fifty, but in reality, my mom is seventy-seven. I am very grateful to God for working so long and so patiently to help me pull away the self-doubt, insecurity, and anger in my closet to find the fear that lay there like an animal waiting to pounce. Facing what I was afraid of was the beginning of my healing and liberty. I didn't understand that for years. I thought if I faced what I was afraid of, it would consume me. But when I brought my fears into the light of God's presence, they took on different proportions; they were real and manageable as opposed to the horror of what we don't talk about but dread.

Perhaps you are able to see yourself in some of these fears: *I am afraid of being hurt, physically. I am afraid of making anyone angry in case they turn on me. I am afraid of being rejected. I am afraid that if I love someone, I give them the power to destroy me.*

These were my fears. But when I brought each one of them before God and looked at them, they changed. In the light of His truth, they did not appear as daunting. I was able to see that my fear of physical violence was left over from my childhood encounters with my dad, and it was not reasonable to still carry that with me every day. I began to understand that someone can be angry with you, and that is okay. I can listen and evaluate what they have said. If it has merit, I can do something about it; if not, I can let it go. I accepted that God will never reject me or leave me. I realized I could choose to have relationships with people whose character revealed integrity rather than choosing people I knew would let me down. I began to make peace with the truth that loving someone always carries an element of risk, but there is no other way to live. Being in relationship opens us up to the possibility of pain, but if we love God and are resting in His grace, pain will not destroy us. The alternative is to live a safe, lonely life.

The veil of fear that hangs in our closet can be brought under the lordship of Jesus Christ as He teaches us how to walk before Him with open hands, trusting that He is in control and He loves us.

I was struck by one of Yoda's lines in the final *Star Wars* movie, *Revenge of the Sith:* "The fear of loss is a path to the dark side. Train yourself to let go of everything you fear to lose."

We are not asked to train ourselves to let go of everything we are afraid to lose, but rather train ourselves by God's grace and the power of the Holy Spirit to bring all our fears to our Father. Our worry will not change the future; it will only rob us of joy in the present.

But what if the thing we are most afraid to lose is the mask that we wear? Perhaps we have worn the mask for so long that we don't know who we are underneath it.

A Look in the Mirror

What are the things that you are most afraid of?

Do you struggle with the what-ifs?

Have past events caused you to carry fear into the present?

Does being in control make you feel safer?

A Closet Prayer

Father,

I confess that at times I am overwhelmed by fear. Sometimes I don't even understand where it is coming from. Teach me to bring my fears to You.

In Jesus' name,

Amen.

Six

Masks:

I'm afraid to be seen

DOROTHY: *Oh . . . you're a very bad man!*
WIZARD: *Oh, no, my dear—I'm—I'm a very good man.*
I'm just a very bad Wizard.

—L. FRANK BAUM (1856–1919), *THE WIZARD OF OZ*

> LORD, *answer me quickly,*
> *because I am getting weak.*
> *Don't turn away from me,*
> *or I will be like those who are dead.*
> *Tell me in the morning about your love,*
> *because I trust you.*
> *Show me what I should do,*
> *because my prayers go up to you.*
> LORD, *save me from my enemies;*
> *I hide in you.*
>
> —PSALM 143:7–9 (NCV)

I had been excited for weeks and now it was *the* day. Mom, Stephen, Frances, and I were in Edinburgh for our summer vacation and tonight we had tickets to see the movie *The Wizard of Oz*. Mom had

seen it before and told me that it was one of the most visually spectacular films ever made. I had high hopes, but as I sat there with
my bag of malt balls and my diet soda and the movie began, my
heart sank.

"She isn't coming yet, Toto. Did she hurt you?"

I nudged my mom, "This is terrible!"

"No, the dog will be fine," she replied, assuming my concern
was for Toto.

"I'm not talking about the dog, Mom; I'm talking about the
movie!"

"It just started."

"But Mom, it's in black and white," I moaned. "That's as visually spectacular as a dead parrot!"

"Just you wait!" she whispered.

So wait I did, and I held my breath as a tornado picked up the house
with Dorothy and Toto in it and sent it spinning through the air. When
it finally crashed to the ground, and Dorothy opened the door and
stepped out into the multicolored, *visually spectacular* Munchkinland,
I could have cried, but my mouth was full of chocolate, so I just looked
at Mom and grinned as much as I could without dribbling.

I love *The Wizard of Oz*. I have watched it over and over, and
each time I am touched by something new. The one element that
soars above all others, though, is the friendship among Dorothy,
the Scarecrow, the Tin Man, and the Cowardly Lion. Through their
commitment to help Dorothy find her way back to Kansas, they are
all changed. They imagine that if they can make it to the Emerald
City and meet the Great Oz, then he will be able to give them what
they need.

Instead, it's the journey itself that changes them. The Scarecrow
discovers that he has a brain as he uses it to help his friends; the Tin
Man finds out that he is all heart; and that Cowardly old Lion finds

the nerve after all. Each of the four characters who travel together down the Yellow Brick Road is honest and vulnerable with one another. They don't hide what they are lacking in their lives.

That's how I see our core team at Women of Faith. We are in our tenth year together, and the journey has changed us all. We bring different strengths and struggles to the mix.

Patsy Clairmont is a brilliant storyteller. When she walks up onto the platform, she comes alive. She is a Rembrandt with words. The pictures she paints are so vivid and beautiful. But her journey to the stage has been a costly one. She struggled for years with agoraphobia and was literally housebound. Physically, Patsy doesn't have much stamina and is the quietest of the group off stage. It is still hard for her to travel sometimes. Her husband, Les, has diabetes and heart problems. They have been married for forty-three years, and many weekends I know she would rather just stay home and be with him.

Marilyn Meberg has two master's degrees, one in English and one in psychology. She is wise and wonderful. She is also the team shrink! Whenever one of us has an issue that is troubling us, we talk to Marilyn. Some of her grace and compassion comes out of loss. Her husband, Ken, died when he was fifty-one of pancreatic cancer, and she lost a fifteen-day-old baby girl to spina bifida.

At her book table, Thelma Wells always has a line of people who just want a hug. She is that kind of woman. She is full of empathy and love from having endured a lot of pain in her life. She was rejected by her mother as a little girl and raised by her great-grandmother. She has tasted the bitter waters of racial prejudice and yet has not become bitter herself.

Luci Swindoll is one of a kind! She worked for over thirty years in the corporate world as an executive with Mobile Oil. She is an artist, a photographer, a musician, a world traveler, and one of the dearest friends that I have. As I write, Luci is about to turn seventy-three—

not one of us would believe it if her birthdate weren't on her driver's license. She is perennially young at heart. Luci has never married and is a compelling example of one who lives life to the fullest every single day. Her home tells the story of her life. The walls are covered with paintings and posters that she has collected from all around the world. Her library shelves are packed with books and journals that she has kept since she was a child. I watch her walk down the few steps from the stage back to her chair and see how much it costs her physically. Luci has trouble with her knees, and at times, the pain is acute.

Nicole Johnson is our team dramatist. Her dramas give words to those who are unable to voice what is in their heads and hearts. Whether she portrays the pain of being diagnosed with breast cancer or the experience of infertility, she brings understanding and companionship to the lonely roads that many women find themselves on.

As you can see, we are a mixed bunch. We are grandmas and professors, businesswomen and the mother of a third-grade child.

More than all of that, we are a team. Instead of entering the arena only when it's our turn to speak, we are all there, all the time. We sit on a row of chairs at the bottom of the steps leading up to the platform. We call it "the porch." We call out to each other if we forget our train of thought and pass snacks and tissues back and forth all weekend.

That's the kind of love Dorothy and her friends find in each other. They discover a porch of pals who will be there through thick and thin. And when they finally arrive at the Emerald City, they discover that the only one wearing a mask is the Great Oz himself. At first glance, the image of the Wizard projected onto the screen in front of Dorothy is impressive and overwhelming, but once Toto pulls back the curtain, she sees that the Great Oz is just an old man speaking into a microphone. Dorothy is very disappointed, but when she tells the Wizard that he is a bad man, his reply is wonderful.

WIZARD: *Oh no, my dear—I'm—I'm a very good man. I'm just a very bad Wizard.*

Just Very Bad Wizards

I have experienced my own *very bad Wizard* moments. I don't know your story or what events have brought you to the place where you are today, but I wonder if you have felt that way too? I wonder if you have worked so hard to keep all the smoke and mirrors going, all the plates spinning in the air, trying to be more than you are able, and then suddenly, they all come crashing down at your feet. I believe that these moments are gifts from God if we will see His hand in them.

They can be the beginning of a new way to live if we will let the masks fall. I have written extensively about my experience with clinical depression in my book, *Honestly,* and have touched on it in *The Heartache No One Sees,* so I will not dwell on it here. But in case we are new friends, let me just give you a brief look at how God delivered me from being a very bad Wizard, a very exhausted Wonder Woman, into a very grateful woman who finally understood that she was wonderfully made.

The Beginning of the End

I had lived in Virginia Beach for almost five years and was happy to be living near the ocean again. I had grown up by the water and find it peaceful and settling even when I don't feel very peaceful inside. I had learned to avoid the more popular main beach and found my own little quiet spot away from the crowds. I sat on the beach one evening and looked out at the waves crashing onto the shore. They seemed to symbolize what was happening in my life. Everything I had ever counted on to give me my identity was drawing to a close.

Tomorrow morning, I would cohost my last edition of *The 700 Club,* and then I would drive to Washington, D.C., and check myself in as a patient in a psychiatric hospital. This was my greatest fear about to be realized. If I had been diagnosed with something physical, I could have easily shared it with others, received support, and persevered. A diagnosis of severe clinical depression, however, was not something to share. I was so ashamed.

For years, I had found my identity in trying to be the perfect Christian woman. I worked hard, I tried to help as many people as I could, I was never late for anything, and nothing was too much trouble. I even had help with my mask. Every morning, I would sit down in the makeup room, and Debbie would do her best to disguise the dark shadows under my eyes. When she had finished with my makeup, she fixed my hair. Aileen would have my suit pressed, hanging beside the right shoes and jewelry. I would take a last look in the mirror and walk down the corridor to Pat Robertson's dressing room where we would pray with the producers before the show each morning. I looked the part, but inside I was slipping further and further into a black hole.

I had tried to save myself, but I couldn't. I had fasted and prayed, exercised, and taken enough vitamins to reenergize a herd of ailing buffalos. In desperation, I talked to my friend Dr. Henry Cloud, and Henry told me that I needed to get help and get it soon. He put me in touch with the right doctor and hospital and arranged for me to be admitted the following evening.

How Much Will It Cost?

I don't remember much about that final show, but I do remember a final conversation. One of my friends who had been with the show for many years and was a respected and loved member of the staff asked me to reconsider. "If you do this, Sheila, no one will trust you again. It will get out that you've been in a psych ward, and it will follow you for the rest of your life."

I was sure she was right, but I had no other choice. I was in so much pain and distress that I decided whatever happened, it couldn't be worse than living like this. After the show, I changed into blue jeans and a sweater, and drove out the front gates of the Christian Broadcasting Center. I was saying goodbye to everything that I thought was important. I had a good job that I loved and was good at. My colleagues trusted and respected me. I had no idea what the future would hold for me or if I even had one.

For those of you who are unfamiliar with this disease, depression is not feeling sorry for yourself or having a few bad days. It is a very real illness that occurs in the brain when certain chemicals necessary for the brain to function well are missing. It is a very treatable disease, but unfortunately, many people do not get help because, like me, they are ashamed to admit that they need it. It is a disease that affects the whole family—the one who suffers and those they love, who often don't understand and don't know what to do to help.

I have many memories of the month I spent in the hospital, but there are two that stand out for me in particular.

What Are You Doing Here?

I didn't sleep well that first night. I felt sick and afraid and alone. At about seven in the morning, I pulled my bathrobe over my pajamas and wandered along the corridor to the patients' lounge. There were six or seven patients there, chatting to each other and drinking decaffeinated coffee. When I walked in, they became silent. Every one of them stopped what they were doing and stared at me. At first, I had no idea why they were staring, and then I suddenly realized that being in a unit run by Christian doctors, there was a very good chance that they had seen *The 700 Club*. I hadn't thought of that possibility until I invaded their space, and the dynamic of the room changed. I didn't know what to say, so I said nothing.

Finally, a man broke the silence. "Are you Sheila Walsh?"

"Yes."

"The one on television?"

"Yes."

"We watch you in here; you're supposed to be helping us."

Talk About a Very Bad Wizard Moment!

I will never forget that moment. Within that split second of mask-dropping, failure was an invitation from God to start a new life, and I took it. All I could say was, "Sorry, I need help too."

I need help too—four words, just four little words that seemed to have the power to cut the burden I had been carrying for so long and let it fall to the ground. In that moment of publicly acknowledging that I was not Wonder Woman or the Great Oz, I found out that it is quite enough just to be human. God is not diminished by our humanity, and no one is helped by our feigned deity either.

There was another moment that profoundly impacted me and showed what God will do if we will take our masks off.

An Answer to Prayer

I had been in the hospital for almost two weeks and was making great strides in searching through my internal closet for all the stuff I had hidden in there for years. I felt like a child bringing her broken dolls to the One who could fix them for her. After supper one evening, I went to the nurses' station to check out my hair dryer. Anything that is potentially dangerous to patients is kept locked up in the "sharps" box, but it can be signed out for a short amount of time.

As I approached the desk, I saw that they were admitting a new patient who was very upset, so I decided to come back later. As I turned to walk away, the new patient's two daughters recognized me and began to cry. Instinctively, I approached them. When their mother looked up and saw me, she threw her arms around my neck and held on tight. She was a faithful *700 Club* viewer who desperately needed help but was very ashamed of her need. God put her there at the same time as me to let her know that she was not alone, and it is all right to get help.

I learned that night that when we take our masks off, we can recognize each other's pain. When we are willing to stand in our brokenness and let the light of Christ shine through, the good news is preached to the poor in spirit, the blind can see the truth, and the lame and wounded can walk again.

> Praise be to the God and Father of our Lord Jesus Christ. God is the Father who is full of mercy and all comfort. He comforts us every time we have trouble, so when others have trouble, we can comfort them with the same comfort God gives us. We share in the many sufferings of Christ. In the same way, much comfort comes to us through Christ. If we have troubles, it is for your comfort and salvation, and if we have comfort, you also have comfort. This helps you to accept patiently the same sufferings we have. Our hope for you is strong, knowing that you share in our sufferings and also in the comfort we receive.
> —2 Corinthians 1:3–7 (NCV)

I don't know what masks you are wearing. I don't know why you feel that you need them. I do know that if by the grace of God you are able to take them off, you will never pick them up again. It may well cost you; it did me, but it was worth it. I had a few moments when people told me that they were disappointed in me, particularly because I still take medication for depression. But I understand this and am fine with it. I don't need the approval of everyone I meet. I have the overwhelming love of my Father and the companionship of others who are having the fabric of their lives lovingly restored by the Master Dressmaker.

But if you have ever made significant changes in your life, you understand that when we shift, everything around us shifts, too, most significantly of all, our relationships.

A Look in the Mirror

Can you identify masks that you wear in your life?
Why do you think you wear them?
What would it cost you to take them off?

A Closet Prayer

Dear Father,

I don't want to hide from You or from those You have placed in my life. Please help me to identify the masks I hide behind and give me the grace and strength to lay them at Your feet.

In Jesus' name,
Amen.

Seven

Broken Relationships:
I want to exchange my family for a new one!

Teacher, which command in the law is the most important?

Jesus answered, "'Love the Lord your God with all your heart, all your soul, and all your mind.' This is the first and most important command. And the second command is like the first: 'Love your neighbor as you love yourself.' All the law and the writings of the prophets depend on these two commands."

—MATTHEW 22:36–40 (NCV)

Father to small boy, "Why are you crying, son?"

Son to father, "The Sunday school teacher prayed that we would be raised in godly families, but I want to stay with you guys."

—ANONYMOUS

I lived in America for over twenty years as a resident alien. "Resident alien" is an intriguing title and quite fitting for a believer. In a sense, all of us who are in relationship with Jesus Christ are resident aliens. We live here, but it gets clearer every day that this is not our home. I don't, however, think that's what the INS had in mind when I was awarded that status.

When Barry and I married in 1994 and took our first trip to Scotland as a married couple, I realized that we must go through different channels in the customs hall. Even though I had a green card, I still had a U.K. passport and Barry had a U.S. passport. We went to our separate lines and met up again in baggage claim with no complications. Then in 1996, Christian was born. Just before Christian turned two years old, we decided to visit his grandma in Scotland. When we got to customs and immigration in London and Christian realized that he and Daddy were in one line and Mommy was at the other end of the hall, he was not thrilled and shared that sentiment quite freely with all around.

The experience bothered me and made me consider applying for citizenship, but it took one more event to catapult me into becoming an American citizen—watching an old movie. As Christian lay fast asleep one evening, I watched a movie about an aircraft that had been hijacked by terrorists. The attackers separated the frightened passengers into two groups: those who held U.S. passports and all others. That was all it took to motivate me into immediate action. If we were going down, we were going down together!

Becoming a citizen is quite a lengthy procedure. There is the initial paperwork, then fingerprinting, and finally an appointment for a personal interview and civics test. I went online to the test site and downloaded one hundred possible questions about history, politics, and general knowledge. We lived in Nashville at the time, and my interview was in Memphis, a three-hour drive away. When the day arrived, Barry and Christian, who was then six, came with me and quizzed me the whole trip.

"Who wrote 'The Star-Spangled Banner'?"

"Francis Scott Key."

"How many stars are on the American flag?"

"Fifty."

"What are the three branches of government?"

"Executive, legislative, and judicial."

"Who was the second president of the United States?"

"Donald Duck—just kidding!"

National Citizen's Day

Well, I am happy to report that I got 100 percent on my test, so all that I needed next was notification of the day that I would take my oath of citizenship. It happened to fall on National Citizen's Day, and I had the honor of joining a small group who swore allegiance to America on the grounds of the Hermitage, the home of former President Andrew Jackson.

It's a day I will never forget. I cried through the oath, and the speeches, and the lunch! I am unabashedly proud to be an American. I love this nation. I love its people and its history, the hope and opportunity afforded to those who are willing to work hard and dream big, but I have to tell you something that few people know: I still privately live in a wee Scottish world!

Every morning when I get up, I put on a pot of coffee, take Belle out to do her doggy duty, and then I sit down at my desk and tune into *Good Morning, Scotland* on my computer. I love it! It's possible now through high-speed Internet connections to access radio programs from around the world. Even though Scotland is six hours ahead, I hit the replay button, and I hear a lovely voice say, "Good morning, Scotland. It is now 6:00 AM and it's a wee bit rainy here in Glasgow today." It's these small things that make me very happy, as if I still have one half of my kilt in bonnie Scotland!

Scottish people are fairly conservative, not very demonstrative or emotional, so it was quite a surprise when I first came to America and discovered how open and communicative many Americans are. When I became a daily presence on television, it was even more overt.

I remember standing in the check-out line in a supermarket when the woman in front of me turned round and, recognizing me, threw her arms around me as if I was her long-lost cousin. I was quite surprised! But cultural styles don't always reveal what is going on under the surface. You can have a nation of quiet, reserved people and a nation of exuberant, outgoing people and find that just beneath the surface they are struggling with the very same things. Broken relationships are one of the greatest casualties of the disastrous choices made in Eden.

Trouble in Paradise

"And Adam called his wife's name Eve, because she was the mother of all living" (Gen. 3:20 NKJV). I mentioned in a previous chapter that Adam's choice of a name for his wife seems generous and hopeful, considering what her disobedience had cost both of them. There is, however, a clear prophetic significance in the choice. By that I mean, at times, God speaks through our human choices and tells a bigger story than we are aware of in that moment. Adam had no way of knowing that through their line would come the Messiah who would undo the curse of Eden and restore life to all who would call on His name.

When Adam and Eve ate from the tree of knowledge of good and evil, they discovered that *they* were evil. What a shock to those made in the perfect image of God to suddenly look at their reflections and see that they were twisted and dark. They become aware of the darkness not only in themselves but also in each other. Eve had originally appeared perfect to Adam, but now he saw her as hostile and accusing. Adam had been the perfect man, but now he looked flawed and weak. What a tragedy!

We experience tension in all our relationships, but not to the extent they did. We have never known a flawless bond. Even so, it seems the memory of Eden is in our DNA, and we still long for perfection. We still think it might be possible to find the flawless relationship.

Enmity

To the serpent, God says that He will place "enmity" between him and the woman, between his seed and hers. That enmity impacts every one of us. It has impacted our culture, our families, every one of our relationships. You feel it every day even if you don't know what to call it. The serpent's seed is our fallen humanity and rebellion, and the woman's seed is the redemption that comes through Christ.

We live in a world that is openly hostile to God and to His holiness. You can't turn on the television or read the newspaper and not feel the strain of the enmity between the god of this world and our Father in heaven. Think about your relationships. Whether it's a husband or child or coworker, every day we have exchanges where we choose to use the language of the redeemed or the language of the fallen. We choose whether we will offer the language of those exiled from the Garden or the language of those on a journey home to heaven.

In each conversation or exchange, the enmity that God spoke of in the Garden is present and possible. Left to our own devices, we will choose the language of the fallen; it's what comes naturally to us. When we become defensive or offended or allow our anger to become out of control, we are embracing the enmity spoken of in Genesis. But we find the grace of God when we realize we are not left to our own devices. God offers the power of the Holy Spirit to choose to live and love differently.

I discovered in my own life that all the new lessons I learned in the hospital were much easier to live out within those four walls, but when I reentered the world outside, I had to deal with shame and fear and anger in relationship with others. I could be godly if it weren't for other people, and when I married, I suddenly found a whole new family to contend with!

The Origin of Mother-in-Law Jokes!

A man brought his dog into the vet and said, "Could you please cut my dog's tail off?"

The vet examined the tail and said, "There is nothing wrong. Why would you want this done?"

The man replied, "My mother-in-law is coming to visit, and I don't want anything in the house to make her think that she is welcome!"

If Eve was the very first mother-in-law, I guess we can trace the first mother-in-law joke back to Cain's wife. But really, it's not a joke. Relationships can be very painful as they show us not only what is in the heart of another but more poignantly, what is in our own heart. I found that out with Eleanor, my mother-in-law.

When Barry and I were dating, we flew into Charleston, South Carolina, where his parents lived, a few times. I got on well with William and Eleanor. Barry is an only child, so they were not used to sharing him with anyone else, but they made me feel welcome in their family. After our wedding, however, we went through some rough seas.

Eleanor was used to Barry confiding in her, but now he confided in me. She was used to driving out to see him as often as she wanted or popping in without warning, but now trips required advanced planning. This was very hard for her to accept. Into this unsettling time for Eleanor came some bitter news.

When Christian was about a year old, Eleanor was diagnosed with liver cancer. The doctors told her that her life expectancy was between six months and two years. We were all devastated by the news, but I was equally surprised by her next request. She asked if she and William could travel with us every weekend to Women of Faith events and take care of Christian. I have to admit my heart sank at the thought, and I tried to deflect her offer by saying, "But, Mom, you have your chemotherapy schedule. I'm sure our dates will conflict."

She replied, "Sheila, if you knew that you had at most two years to live, would you want to spend it on a drip or with those you love? I can ask the doctor to plan my therapy around your trips."

And so we agreed that they would travel with us. Most weekends it was great, but every now and again, we would have a very difficult weekend. I know now that she was afraid and sad, but it came out as anger toward me, and I couldn't see behind the words to the wounded heart. Instead of pressing in and trying to help her, I pulled back defensively. When I think back on that time, I wish I had understood that her angry words were a cry for help and connection, but I didn't.

It was only as she became bedridden in the last few weeks of her life that we began to hear each other. I remember sitting in bed with her one night after I had given her some morphine to ease the pain. I had my arm around her, and she had her head on my shoulder. I thought she was asleep, and so I quietly began to sing the hymn "Great Is Thy Faithfulness." It was one of the hymns I knew she loved. Suddenly, in the midst of the song, she said, "Sheila, I never meant any of those things I said. I just felt so alone and afraid. I didn't know how to say that, so it came out wrong."

I understand that all too well. I have chosen anger to cover my fear or shame. When Adam and Eve spoke to each before the Fall, their words were unambiguous, crystal clear, and true, but then the waters became muddy. Just as they lost the ability to speak without their brokenness intervening, so have we. Our great hope is that Christ offers us a way to *choose* now what was natural for Adam and Eve in the beginning.

I Am Sorry

I don't deal well with things that seem petty. If someone takes offense over something that seems silly to me, I can run out of grace quickly.

A friend of mine was upset about a decision I made over a past writing project. It made no sense to me. It didn't affect her in any way that I could see. We don't see each other very often, but we met up while I was writing this book, and it became clear that she was frustrated with me. My first instinct was to say, *"This is really stupid,"* but I have learned to corral those first instincts, particularly the ones I feel an urgency to share.

The more I feel—*I need to tell her this now!*—the more I need to hold back and wait. I didn't say anything that day to her, but I did talk to God about it. I told Him that it made no sense to me at all. Even as I was talking to God, I could feel my emotions stirring. I was getting mad, and I felt an old tendency to back away from relationship resurfacing. I lay in bed that night, thinking, *Well, I'm glad that conversation was just between the Lord and me.*

The next morning, I realized that I couldn't talk to her if I had any expectations about her response. I could only do it if my heart was for her and her well-being. When we had a moment alone, I told her how sorry I was that a decision I had made had hurt her. I told her that had never been in my heart and that I loved her. She accepted that with grace and let it go.

I can't tell you what a huge weight was lifted off my shoulders. I hate being out of fellowship with a friend. I didn't apologize for my decision because I knew it was the right one for me; I just expressed my concern that it had hurt her. I believe that is a key to peace in many of our relationships. Previously, I had seen two paths ahead that I could choose from: (1) I could express my frustration, tell how silly I thought any particular issue was, and disregard the feelings of another; (2) I could apologize for the right decision and change it just so that no one would be upset with me.

Now I saw that I could stand by what I believed to be right but still care about how it might impact another whether it made sense to me or not.

> Love suffers long *and* is kind; love does not envy; love does not parade itself, is not puffed up; does not behave rudely, does not seek its own, is not provoked, thinks no evil; does not rejoice in iniquity, but rejoices in the truth; bears all things, believes all things, hopes all things, endures all things.
> —1 Corinthians 13:4–7 (NKJV)

No matter how well we think that we know someone, we never know their full story. Sometimes their responses to us can have roots in past disappointment. Disappointment can so easily become bitterness. God invites us to bring our disappointment out of the closet and expose it to the light of His love and grace.

A Look in the Mirror

As you look at your closest relationships, where do you see the most tension?

What do you think that exposes in you?

How do you think you could make some changes that would enable you to choose the language of the redeemed instead of the language of the fallen?

A Closet Prayer

Father God,

I ask for Your grace and mercy on me and in all my relationships. Teach me to bring my anger and fear to You so that grace and mercy will cover my words to others.

Amen.

Eight

Disappointment:
I don't know what happened to my dreams

When Abigail saw David, she quickly got off her donkey and bowed facedown on the ground before him. She fell at David's feet and said, "My master, let the blame be on me! Please let me talk to you. Listen to what I say. My master, don't pay attention to this worthless man Nabal. He is like his name. His name means 'fool,' and he is truly a fool. But I, your servant, didn't see the men you sent."

—1 SAMUEL 25:23–25 (NCV)

For of all sad words of tongue or pen,
The saddest are these: "It might have been!"

—JOHN GREENLEAF WHITTIER (1807–1892), *MAUD MULLER*

I have a feeling that Abigail's father chose her name when he looked into the eyes of this little one after she was born. It means "father rejoices." As he watched her grow into a beautiful and kind girl, it was clear, too, that she had a rich wit and strong convictions. It must have been on his mind and heart to look for the perfect husband for such a woman.

She was always respectful of her elders, honoring to her father

71

and the other men in the tribe, but it was known by many that if you wanted a clearheaded opinion on a difficult situation, ask Abigail.

Nabal seemed like a good choice. We read in 1 Samuel 25 that Nabal was very rich. He had three thousand sheep and a thousand goats. Perhaps like many dads, Abigail's father wanted her to marry someone who would be able to take good care of her and provide for her, but the choice was a disastrous one.

A Disappointing Choice

Nabal was an evil, cruel, and callous man. I wonder how long it took for Abigail to encounter that side of his nature? We know that she was beautiful, so perhaps for a while, things were fine at home, but he was a heavy drinker, and when he was drunk, he became a different person. My heart ached for her as I read the story.

How disappointing it must have been to realize that she was tied for the rest of her life to a man who was brutal and stupid. In nature, he was the antithesis of Abigail. It's clear later in her story as she encountered King David that Abigail was raised in a godly home. She was familiar with the teachings of the prophets. That knowledge and her heart not only saved her life but also the lives of her entire household. I believe that as we unfold her story, we will understand how to position our lives when disappointment floods our hearts.

> She possessed in harmonious combination these two qualities which are valuable to anyone, but which are essential to one who has to manage men—the tact of a wise wife and the religious principles of a good woman.[1]

Every weekend, as I travel and speak to women, I meet those who are living with a Nabal or living with the crushing weight of disappointment and what might have been; perhaps you are too.

Why, Lord?

To protect the anonymity of the women whose stories I want to highlight, I have changed the names, a few of the irrelevant details, and kept the pertinent points.

Susan

Susan was raised in a good Christian home. It was important to her that she should remain a virgin until she was married. This was not a popular choice at her high school. But as a young girl, Susan had begun the habit of committing God's Word to memory. When she was struggling to keep to her commitment, she would dig deep into her heart and mind and pull it up:

> Happy are those who don't listen to the wicked,
>   who don't go where sinners go,
>   who don't do what evil people do.
> They love the LORD's teachings,
>   and they think about those teachings day and night.
> They are strong, like a tree planted by a river.
>   The tree produces fruit in season,
>   and its leaves don't die.
> Everything they do will succeed. —Psalm 1:1–3 (NCV)

When she met Peter, it seemed to all that it was a match made in heaven. He was charming and witty, respectful to Susan's parents, and he had a good job teaching high-school English. He even taught the junior-high Sunday school. They were married two years after they met.

At first things seemed to be as she hoped, but after a few months Susan noticed that Peter came to bed later and later every night. Their sex life had suffered considerably because of this, and that concerned and hurt her. One night, she woke up, it was two o'clock, and Peter was not in bed. She grabbed her robe and went downstairs. He wasn't in the kitchen, so she got a glass of milk from the refrigerator and went into his office. What she saw sickened her. The images on the computer screen were unlike anything she had ever seen or imagined. Susan had heard of men addicted to online pornography but never dreamed that it would invade her marriage too. *How could this happen to me? Why would God let this happen when I've kept myself pure? How can I talk to anyone about something so shameful? How can I ever let him touch me again?*

Anne

Anne had a very different upbringing than Susan. Her parents were not believers although they took her to Sunday school. When she started high school, she dropped out of the youth group because her new friends had no interest in church. She first slept with a boy when she was fifteen. She knew that she was in love with him, but he quickly lost interest in her.

She was heartbroken, but the experience hardened her heart too. She had several more relationships after that, and in college, she became pregnant. The boy had no interest in her or the baby. Anne went with a friend and had an abortion. She told herself that this was the responsible thing to do even though her decision haunted her. One night, a friend invited her to a concert. She had never heard of the artist. It became apparent early on in the concert that he was a Christian. She wondered if she could slip out, but she was in the middle of a row, and it would have been difficult.

Her heart was thumping in her chest as she listened to the words of the songs. They promised what had been missing for as long as she could remember—peace, love, and hope. That Sunday, Anne found a church near campus and went. The people were friendly and kind. She wondered what their response would be if she ever told her secret. She signed up for a weekend retreat for women, and during that time in a small, intimate group, Anne told her story. Through tears that had been building up for so long, she gave her heart and life to Christ.

For the first time in her life, she felt free and full of hope, but her hope was short-lived. During a routine physical, she learned that she was infected with the HIV virus. *Why now, God? Why did You let me find peace and hope just to take it away? Is this Your punishment for aborting the baby?*

The Faces of Disappointment

Disappointment is a crushing blow to the soul and can take many forms. Nave's Topical Bible Index defines it as "the non-fulfillment of one's hopes."[2]

Disappointment can be when the children you have raised in the faith walk away. Eli the priest knew what that tasted like. In 1 Samuel 2:12 (NCV) we read, "Now Eli's sons were evil men; they did not care about the LORD." That is a devastating blow to a parent who loves and honors God.

Disappointment can result from a personal failure. The psalmist David knew that, "I know about my wrongs, and I can't forget my sin" (Ps. 51:3 NCV). It can lead to disappointment and disillusionment with your own life. When regret is allowed to fester and give birth to hopelessness, it can have disastrous consequences.

A Wasted Life

We see that in the life of the man Ahithophel. The Bible doesn't tell us much about him. We know that he was King David's advisor until David committed adultery with Bathsheba. Then he switched allegiance to David's son Absalom, who was in revolt against his father. Ahithophel advised Absalom to pursue and kill David immediately. He believed that David's sin was so great that he had lost his right to rule over God's people. He counted David out, but God hadn't. Have you ever felt that way about someone? *How can You still use her after she sinned? Why would You give her that opportunity? She doesn't deserve it; I do.*

Righteous indignation is a powerful force. When it is used in the service of God, it can produce tremendous results, but when turned against God, it is deadly.

A new advisor entered Absalom's camp. His name was Hushai. Hushai was loyal to David but hoped to discover what Absalom's plans were and use his influence to change them. The two men offered their advice: (1) kill David now; (2) wait and see what transpires.

Absalom took Hushai's advice and waited, thereby giving David time to rebuild his army. Absalom was killed in battle, and David's kingdom was left intact. Ahithophel felt as if his whole life had been a waste. We read, "When Ahithophel saw that the Israelites did not accept his advice, he saddled his donkey and went to his hometown. He left orders for his family and property, and then he hanged himself"(2 Sam. 17:23 NCV).

Disappointment hits at the very core of who we are. It affects our pride, our belief in fair play, and our sense of entitlement. It rips at our dreams, our hopes, our very vision of what makes life worth living. Most of us would not resort to the extreme measures that Ahithophel took, but we experience death in another way. It feels as if part of who we are has died.

One of my friends confessed to me that she had struggled with my involvement with Women of Faith. She has longed to be a writer and speaker and knew that when I was on *The 700 Club*, I was given many enviable opportunities. Then I disappeared from the public radar as I received treatment for depression. When I was invited in 1996 to join Women of Faith, it just didn't seem fair to her. I had my chance; now it should be hers.

I understood her frustration and admired her honesty. I've had several well-known women tell me that they don't think our team is as powerful as it could be. They say that there are better speakers or younger speakers, and it should be their turn now. We would probably all agree with that, but it is irrelevant.

God is the One who decides whom He will use at any given moment. It doesn't say anything about us; it says a lot about Him. He uses the most unlikely, broken people so that it is clear to all around, God is in control.

Worn Down by God's People

Sometimes God's appointed leaders can grow so disappointed with God's people that their lives arrive at, what would seem to us, an untimely end.

In the south of London, Metropolitan Tabernacle sits across from a run-down subway station. It is off the tourist path, and average Sunday attendance hovers at three hundred. That might seem an insignificant number to Americans who have grown used to the mega church, but it is a healthy number for the United Kingdom.

Metropolitan Tabernacle's successful ministry attracts young people and serves a vital need in the inner city. Its most famous minister was Charles Spurgeon. On June 7, 1891, Charles Spurgeon preached there for the last time. He was exhausted in ministry and broken down by denominational conflict. His hair was white, his face lined, his heavy frame weak. He ended his sermon without knowing these would be his last words in the pulpit: "His service is life, peace, joy. Oh, that you would enter on it at once! God help you to enlist under the banner of Jesus even this day! Amen!"

That afternoon Spurgeon became ill. He lay in bed for more than a month, most of the time unconscious, then rallied enough in late summer for a trip to the south of France. But about midnight January 31, 1892, Spurgeon breathed his last breath. He was only fifty-seven.[3]

We know that God's timing is perfect, but I wonder how many godly men and women have so taken the burden of God's work onto their own backs that the weight is just too much to bear?

A Way Out of the Closet of Disappointment

As I read on in Abigail's story, I saw an alternative way to deal with bitter disappointment. She was about to encounter David and have her life changed forever. David was on the run from the wrath of King Saul. He and six hundred of his men were camped out near where Nabal kept his livestock. David's men watched over Nabal's shepherds and made sure that no bandits robbed them or harmed his flocks. It was the custom to return such a favor with provisions to feed the men. David sent word to Nabal and asked for this courtesy to be extended to them, and Nabal refused.

> He answered them, "Who is David? Who is this son of Jesse? Many slaves are running away from their masters today! I have bread and water, and I have meat that I killed for my servants who cut the wool. But I won't give it to men I don't know."
> —1 Samuel 25:10–11 (NCV)

When David heard this, he was furious. His legendary temper kicked into full gear, and he took four hundred of his men, and they set off to slaughter Nabal and all his men. One of Nabal's servants heard what was about to happen, and he came to Abigail and told her what had taken place. She immediately got busy.

> Abigail hurried. She took two hundred loaves of bread, two leather bags full of wine, five cooked sheep, a bushel of cooked grain, a hundred cakes of raisins, and two hundred cakes of pressed figs and put all these on donkeys. —1 Samuel 25:18 (NCV)

When everything was ready, she got on a donkey and went out to intercept David. Can you imagine this one woman facing the wrath of David and four hundred armed men? Abigail got off her donkey and bowed down before David. She asked him to place the blame on her, telling David that it was common knowledge that her husband was a fool. With wisdom and humility she reminded David of who he was:

> The LORD will keep all his promises of good things for you. He will make you leader over Israel. Then you won't feel guilty or troubled because you killed innocent people and punished them. Please remember me when the LORD brings you success. —1 Samuel 25:30–31 (NCV)

David was deeply touched by her, accepted the gifts she brought, and turned his men around. When Abigail arrived home, Nabal was too drunk to hear her story. She told him the next morning, and upon hearing the news, he either had a heart attack or a stroke (the exact malady is unclear) and died ten days later. When David heard that her husband had died, he asked Abigail to marry him.

Here's what I glean from her life. She must have been very disappointed when she realized what kind of man her husband was. I'm sure his behavior was at best rude and at worst abusive, but she didn't let who Nabal was determine who she was. She held on to

God and to the integrity of her own character. The servants loved and respected her. She was the one they came to in times of trouble.

There must have been many moments when she had to pour water on the flash fires that her brute of a husband started. It would have been understandable for Abigail to leave Nabal, but God gave her the grace to stay and the strength to remain true to herself.

There are many modern Abigails. There are those of you who live in very difficult and disappointing situations, but somehow, as you throw yourself on God's mercy, you remain strong and true. I think of the words of Elizabeth Barrett Browning as I salute you:

> The world may sound no trumpets, ring no bells;
> The book of life the shining record tells.[4]

A Look in the Mirror

Can you identify the places of disappointment in your life?
How have you dealt with that disappointment?
What can you take from the life of Abigail that will impact your own?

A Closet Prayer

Father God,

I confess my disappointment to You. There are many things in my life and in the lives of others that don't make sense to me. I ask for Your grace to bring my disappointment out of the closet and into Your light.

In Jesus' name,
Amen.

Part Two

Spring Cleaning My Life

Nine

Facing the Truth:

Taking a fearless look in my closet

GLINDA: *You don't need to be helped any longer. You've always had the power to go back to Kansas.*
DOROTHY: *I have?*
SCARECROW: *Then why didn't you tell her before?*
GLINDA: *Because she wouldn't have believed me. She had to learn it for herself.*

—L. FRANK BAUM (1856–1919), *THE WIZARD OF OZ*

So if we say we have fellowship with God, but we continue living in darkness, we are liars and do not follow the truth. But if we live in the light, as God is in the light, we can share fellowship with each other. Then the blood of Jesus, God's Son, cleanses us from every sin.

—1 JOHN 1:6–7 (NCV)

William had lived through the Depression, and the memories of financial struggles were still deep in his heart. As the years passed, he married Eleanor, and they built a lovely home on James Island near Charleston, South Carolina. They wanted a family, but it seemed as if that dream would permanently elude them. They tried for ten years, and then one day, Eleanor received the news she had been waiting for: she was pregnant. When she gave birth to a boy, they named him Barry. He was the delight of their lives, and they spoiled him. The first time I met my future mother-in-law, Eleanor said, "His dad ruined him! It was the red Corvette that did it. We shouldn't have bought him such a flashy car. He's wanted the best of everything since."

Most of this ribbing was in good form or slightly tongue-in-cheek. But I have discovered that my husband is a connoisseur of all things fine. He loves good shoes and elegant furniture. He studies design magazines and picks all my clothes for stage. I'm a mess really. If left to myself, I would stumble up onto the platform in my jeans and a ball cap, but Barry finds just the right outfit, shoes, and jewelry and sends me on my way.

After Eleanor died, we invited William to move to Nashville and live with us. We encouraged him to keep his home in Charleston for a while to see if he liked living with us. He had just lost his wife, and another loss didn't seem wise or necessary. After a few months, he told us that he wanted to sell his home and make the move permanent. We were all thrilled. He was such a sweet, funny man, and Christian adored him.

Before he could sell the house, we had to clean out all the stuff that they had accumulated over the forty-three years they had lived there. William chose a few pieces of furniture that he wanted to keep, and we had those shipped to Nashville. The other furniture was sold.

Everything was going well until we looked in the attic. I have never seen so much stuff squeezed into one place in my life! We drug it all out of the dark attic until there were piles and piles of old newspapers, old coke bottles, over a hundred dolls, fifty pairs of scissors, enough soap to wash the planet, rope, string, almost everything Barry had worn since his birth, and on and on and on.

When I asked William about each item, his response was the same, "That might be a collector's item one day!"

He had a hard time throwing away anything for fear that if times got tough again, he might need something to sell. When we finally had everything out and piled from one end of the upstairs bedroom to the other, William said, "I forgot that all that was in there."

That's the way it goes though, isn't it? We push things to the back and mean to deal with them when we have some spare time, but if you are anything like me, spare time never seems to arrive.

What's in your closet?

It was a Herculean task cleaning out William and Eleanor's attic. When it was finally empty, I saw a piece of string hanging from the roof. I asked William what it was, and he said, "Well, that's the light!"

I pulled the cord and suddenly this dark space that I had been crawling around in was flooded with light. As I watched little critters scurry for cover, I decided that perhaps it had been good that we had cleaned up in the dark.

Not so with our lives. If we honestly want to get rid of any junk in the closets of our souls, we can only do it with the help and illumination of the Holy Spirit. The psalmist David left us wonderful instructions as to where to begin:

> Search me, O God, and know my heart;
> Try me, and know my anxieties;
> And see if *there is any* wicked way in me,
> And lead me in the way everlasting. —Psalm 139:23–24 (NKJV)

The Message interprets the passage this way:

> Investigate my life, O God,
> 　　find out everything about me;

Cross-examine and test me,
>   get a clear picture of what I'm about;
See for yourself whether I've done anything wrong—
>   then guide me on the road to eternal life.
>   —Psalm 139:23–24

I love David's request. He asks God to search his heart where his motives and passions rest. He asks God to search his mind where fear and mistrust can cloud his faith. He asks God to expose any sin and keep him walking straight toward home. That is my prayer as we begin this section of spring cleaning our lives.

I pray that God will show us what is in our hearts. I pray that God will reveal the fear that torments the mind. I pray that God in His mercy will expose any sin so that we can bring it to the Cross and be made clean and whole. I pray that God will help us let go of any unforgiveness, bitterness, or disappointment. I pray that He will fill us with His Holy Spirit so that we may honor Him in all we do.

Why Bother?

You might ask, why bother to dig up old stuff? Why go searching through my internal closet when my life is going well now? In the next chapter, we'll talk about sin. It is clear why sin must be dealt with, but what about old childhood wounds? What about the messages that are still scripted onto our hearts? Can't we just live with them? Absolutely we can. I don't believe that the Lord forces us to deal with things that we don't want to deal with.

My sister, Frances, and I have had many honest conversations about this very thing. Frances has very few memories of our father or how hard it was when he was ill. She is content with that. She has a good marriage, two grown sons, and she loves her job as a teacher. She is very involved in their church where her husband is an elder and sees no need to go raking things up. I understand that.

But I found the stuff in my closet was affecting my life, profoundly. In the weeks leading up to my hospitalization, I read an anonymous quote that haunted me, "When the pain of remaining the same becomes greater than the pain of change, then you will change."

That's where I was. I had no idea what it would cost to take a fearless look at my life, but I was sure that it couldn't be any worse than living the way I was living. I began with a simple prayer that had an intense impact on my life; God took me at my word.

Father,
I don't know what is wrong with me, but I am exhausted. I'm tired in my body and sick at heart. I don't know what to do. Will You please help me?

　　　　　　　　　　　　　　　　　　　　　Amen.

I had tried to fix myself for so long, and I had run out of options. Sometimes that's the best place to be.

I Quit!

Christian is a very loving boy, but he is also independent in a very healthy way. I try to give him as much space to do things by himself as I can. I let him choose what he wants to wear on nonschool days even if the color combination hurts my eyes. He finds it very difficult and frustrating to not be able to do something that he thinks he should be able to do.

We were at a baseball game one night, supporting our local Frisco Roughriders. Lynn Wittenberg, our Women of Faith VP of marketing, had acquired great seats for us. She practically designed the whole park before she left to join the staff of Women of Faith.

Christian strained to catch every fly ball that came into the crowd, and there were many that night, but to no avail. He was getting pretty discouraged until a friend of Lynn's came up, introduced herself, and presented Christian with a baseball signed by all the players. Well! He was over the moon and asked me if we could go to the team store and buy a plastic display case for his new prize possession.

We bought the small case and sat on the ground to put the ball in it. He tried and tried to open it and couldn't. I offered to help, but he said he could do it. After about twenty minutes of muttering, he finally said, "I quit!" I took the case from him and pulled the top off. It was very simple when you knew how to do it but maddeningly complex if you didn't.

I find the same to be true with my life. I struggled in my own power for years, trying to rid myself of fear and shame, of anger and isolation, but it was only when I finally said, "I quit!" that God began to do what He had been longing to do all along.

> Come, Thou Fount of every blessing,
> Tune my heart to sing Thy grace;
> Streams of mercy, never ceasing,
> Call for songs of loudest praise.
> Teach me some melodious sonnet,
> Sung by flaming tongues above.
> Praise the mount! I'm fixed upon it,
> Mount of Thy redeeming love . . .
> O to grace how great a debtor
> Daily I'm constrained to be!
> Let Thy goodness, like a fetter,

Bind my wandering heart to Thee.
Prone to wander, Lord, I feel it,
Prone to leave the God I love;
Here's my heart, O take and seal it,
Seal it for Thy courts above.[1]

A Look in the Mirror

As you look at your life, will you choose to stay the same or do you want God to expose the things that might be holding you back?

What does it feel like to live under such a heavy load?

Can you identify the hardest truth to face about yourself?

A Closet Prayer

Father God,

I pray with Your servant David, "Search me, O God, and know my heart; Try me, and know my anxieties; And see if there is any wicked way in me, And lead me in the way everlasting."

Amen.

Ten

Taking the Trash Out:
Bringing my stuff to Jesus

One of the Pharisees asked Jesus to eat with him, so Jesus went into the Pharisee's house and sat at the table. A sinful woman in the town learned that Jesus was eating at the Pharisee's house. So she brought an alabaster jar of perfume and stood behind Jesus at his feet, crying. She began to wash his feet with her tears, and she dried them with her hair, kissing them many times and rubbing them with the perfume. When the Pharisee who asked Jesus to come to his house saw this, he thought to himself, "If Jesus were a prophet, he would know that the woman touching him is a sinner!"

—LUKE 7:36–39 (NCV)

Jesus! what a Friend for sinners!
Jesus! Lover of my soul;
Friends may fail me, foes assail me,
He, my Savior, makes me whole.

—J. WILBUR CHAPMAN (1859–1918),
"JESUS! WHAT A FRIEND FOR SINNERS!"

I love fresh flowers. Even as a student in London with very little dis-
cretionary income, I set aside enough money for fresh flowers every
week. If I had to skip dinner one evening to afford them, I would
gladly do it. I received more nourishment from the fragrant aroma
of flowers than from any regulation meatloaf.

My favorite flowers are tulips. I lived in Holland for a year after
college, and Dutch tulips are the most beautiful of all. If you ever
find yourself in Europe in the spring, I encourage you to visit
Keukenhof Gardens, just southwest of Amsterdam. Keukenhof
Gardens is known as the world's largest flower garden. It's only
open eight weeks each year, from late March to May, but over
800,000 people visit each season. The beauty of the gardens and the
brilliant bulb flowers just cannot be adequately captured in words.
It is a breathtaking sea of color and grace. Since Keukenhof has
more than seven million spring flowers planted, some type of brilliant bulbs are in bloom the entire season.

When I am choosing flowers for myself, I almost always choose
white. I think a crystal vase with fresh white tulips is a work of art—
pure, elegant, and simple. I catch myself smiling every time I walk
past such an arrangement. At times, even just one single flower displayed in a vase can be beautiful and carry a message all its own.

A Single White Flower

Harold Begbie chronicled the work of the Salvation Army in
London in the early 1900s. He recorded how the lowest of the low
were touched and changed by the love of Christ through the simple
kindnesses of these soldiers of God. One story he wrote tells how the
gift of a single white flower actually changed the life of a woman.

She was a prostitute who had spent years on the streets. One
evening, a young female Salvation Army officer gave her a single

white flower. Begbie writes that as she held the bloom in her hands she said, "I was once white like this flower." She began to weep and confessed her desire to be pure again. One act of kindness in giving this woman a symbol of everything that she felt she was not changed her, and she left her life of prostitution.[1]

Alabaster Boxes

In Luke, we see "a certain woman who was a sinner" so touched by Christ that she turns her life around. I wonder, *what was it that touched this woman so deeply?* Her story depicts a treasure chest of grace and mercy to all who feel ashamed to come to Christ because of their life choices. The Scottish writer Mackintosh Mackay says of Luke's account, "The story bears stamped on its very face the impress of Him who spake as never men spake."[2] Every person in the room that night heard a message that cut through everything that seemed important and right and revealed everything that matters to the heart of God:

> One of the Pharisees asked Jesus to eat with him, so Jesus went into the Pharisee's house and sat at the table. A sinful woman in the town learned that Jesus was eating at the Pharisee's house. So she brought an alabaster jar of perfume and stood behind Jesus at his feet, crying. She began to wash his feet with her tears, and she dried them with her hair, kissing them many times and rubbing them with the perfume. —Luke 7:36–38 (NCV)

What was it that brought this woman to Jesus that night? It was common knowledge that she was a sinner. The Greek word used for *sinner* in this passage suggests sexual sin. It translates as "unchastity," so it is reasonable to assume she was a prostitute. What would make a known prostitute push her way through a judgmental, religious dinner party to get to the feet of Jesus? There is a phrase that crops up in all four gospel records that gives us a clue: "This news about Jesus spread through all Judea and into all the places around there" (Luke 7:17 NCV).

In chapter 6 of Luke, we read of a woman on her way to bury her son. Jesus has compassion on her and brings her son back to life. I'm sure the news of this miracle spread like wildfire so that, by the time Jesus goes to the Pharisee's house for dinner, everyone knows who Jesus is. I imagine this sinful woman, trapped in a lifestyle that is destroying her, decides to take the biggest risk of her life and reach out for help.

I see in her a woman who had reached the point of knowing that the pain of change could not be worse than what she was living with now. I met her modern-day sister, and hearing what God did in her life was one of the most humbling experiences I have had.

Jennifer, Come Home

In our culture, one of the greatest perceptions of evangelical Christians is that we look down on sinners, particularly those engaged in sexual sin. I think that's tragic. Perhaps we imagine that those involved in a very promiscuous lifestyle, with drugs and alcohol, are just having the time of their lives, but I believe that in every human heart there is a cry to be free of the things that bind us and a desire to be loved by God. I discovered that when I met Jennifer, a woman just like the one in Luke's account.

I was writing songs for a new project and working on a song about a modern prodigal daughter. I decided to name the prodigal Jennifer. When the CD was finished, I appeared as a guest on *The 700 Club* one morning and sang the song. I had no idea that God had heard the cry of a real Jennifer and was about to call her by name.

Time to Come Home

Jennifer lived in Los Angeles and was a high-priced call girl. She was beautiful and glamorous. The men who picked her up drove fast, expensive cars and paid her well. But inevitably Jennifer's life began to suffer as she became addicted to drugs and alcohol. Her life began to spiral downward. Then she found out that she had cancer. Her career was built on being beautiful and seductive, and when her looks began to change, her life began to crumble. One night she lay on the floor of her apartment and cried out to God for help. The television was on in the room and as she wept, she heard someone begin to sing,

> Jennifer, come home, we are waiting for you.
> Jennifer, come home, how we miss you.
> For the party can't begin,
> 'til the family's gathered in.
> Jennifer, we miss you.
> Don't you know we love you?
> Jennifer, come home.

Jennifer picked up the phone and dialed the number on the screen. One of *The 700 Club* counselors prayed with her and led her home to Jesus. Some time later, we sent a film crew out to Los Angeles to capture Jennifer's story. Her cancer is now in remission, and she spends her evenings on the streets of LA, sharing the love of God with prostitutes.

As I watched her story when it finally aired, I wept at the goodness and mercy of God to link up a Scottish woman with a simple song and a desperate woman with a broken heart and introduce us at the foot of the Cross where all sinners meet.

Grief and the Washing of Feet

The woman known only as a sinner made her way past those who stared and knelt behind Jesus. Her grief and repentance were such that her tears were able to wash the feet of Jesus. It's a very strange thing that Simon had not made arrangements to have Jesus' feet washed as he came in that night. If it was an oversight, it was huge, and if it was intended as an insult, it was noted. As most people wore open sandals or no shoes at all, it was a common courtesy to offer a bowl of fresh water and a towel at the door. The lowest in the household performed the foot-washing task, but no one had performed it that night.

> Then Jesus turned toward the woman and said to Simon, "Do you see this woman? When I came into your house, you gave me no water for my feet, but she washed my feet with her tears and dried them with her hair. —Luke 7:44 (NCV)

Jesus acknowledged that this woman's sins were many but also pointed out that her repentance and love were great.

More than likely you don't relate to the prostitute or to Jennifer, but there is a key to how we view our sin contained elsewhere in this passage from Luke. As the woman washed his feet, Jesus turned to Simon and began to tell him a story: Two men owed money to a bank, one five hundred coins and one fifty. The bank manager decided to forgive both debts. Which one would be more grateful?

> Simon, the Pharisee, answered, "I think it would be the one who owed him the most money."
>
> Jesus said to Simon, "You are right." Then Jesus turned toward the woman and said to Simon, "Do you see this woman?

When I came into your house, you gave me no water for my feet, but she washed my feet with her tears and dried them with her hair. You gave me no kiss of greeting, but she has been kissing my feet since I came in. You did not put oil on my head, but she poured perfume on my feet. I tell you that her many sins are forgiven, so she showed great love. But the person who is forgiven only a little will love only a little."
—Luke 7:43–47 (NCV)

Let's unpack that a little and apply it to our own lives. I used to be more like Simon than the woman who washed Jesus' feet. As I saw it, I wasn't one of the big sinners. I didn't drink or smoke; I had kept myself pure, at least in body, until I was married. My gratitude and my worship matched my perception.

What I totally missed was that all the sins I had shoved into the back of my closet—the shame, unforgiveness, and anger—were just as potent as those sins that are more obvious. If I had been the only one on this earth, Jesus would still have needed to die to save me. I didn't understand that until I found myself in that little church in Washington, D.C., sitting beside the psychiatric nurse who had accompanied me.

As the pastor spoke that morning, it was as if someone held a mirror up to me, and I saw how I really looked left to my own devices. I saw the blackness in my own heart, the self-righteousness, the self-pity, and shame mixed in a deadly cocktail. That is why I ran to the front of the church and fell at the foot of the Cross and wept. I had no idea if such a display would be frowned upon, but I didn't care. I knew that I needed Jesus, and I knew He was waiting for me. I wept and washed His feet with my tears of grateful repentance.

What's in Your Alabaster Box?

I was proud that I had never engaged in sexual sin, but my thought life was not always pure. I was proud that I had never physically harmed anyone, but my anger had stabbed them in the heart. I was proud that I had never been addicted to drugs or alcohol, but I had abused food and used it to cover my pain.

As I began to bring my trash out of the closet, I wept over the barriers I had covered up between God and myself and between me and others.

I don't know what you might be hiding. It might be alcohol, pain medication, adultery, impure thoughts, bitterness, unforgiveness, self-righteousness . . . the list is long. I just want you to know that if you will bring it to the foot of the Cross, Jesus will take it all and give you a new heart and a clean spirit.

A Look in the Mirror

Which person do you relate to more, Simon or the woman who loved much?

Which sin do you struggle with most?

Are you willing to take the trash out?

A Closet Prayer

Father God,

I confess that I am a sinner. Give me the grace to see the sin that I am blind to and help me bring it to the foot of the Cross. Give me the heart to embrace whoever stands beside me there.

Amen.

Eleven

Timing Is Everything:
Releasing childhood pain

> *I have many issues*
> *I keep them close to me*
> *I'll take them out and show you*
> *I know you'd love to see*
> *They're all I want to talk about*
> *They're all I have to say*
> *Forget* Desperate Housewives
> *You should see my play!*

> —SHEILA WALSH

> *The LORD says, "Forget what happened before,*
>   *and do not think about the past.*
> *Look at the new thing I am going to do.*
>   *It is already happening. Don't you see it?*
> *I will make a road in the desert*
>   *and rivers in the dry land.*

> —ISAIAH 43:18–19 (NCV)

In August of 2004, Barry, Christian, Belle (our bichon frise pup), and I moved from Nashville, Tennessee, to Dallas, Texas. Dallas is a very easy city to fly in and out of, and as so much of our lives are spent on the road, it was a practical choice for us. We also wanted to live close to the rest of the Women of Faith speaker team who live in Dallas.

We arrived at our new home four days before Christian started second grade. I learned very quickly that Dallas traffic is something you have to experience to believe. So I did a trial run the day before school began to see how long it would take me in the morning rush hour. I was glad I did. I discovered the drive that takes about twelve minutes midmorning takes forty-five minutes at seven o'clock.

All the moms and dads were there that first day hovering over their anxious, excited children. Christian's teacher was lovely, very warm, and comforting. Christian sat at his desk, looking very smart in his navy blue shorts and white shirt. (The children in his school wear uniforms, which I appreciate because it seems to stop the competition for who has the trendiest outfit.) When all the children had finally settled, the moms and dads were invited to leave!

The following morning, I dropped Christian off and headed to Starbucks for some coffee. I got back in my car, and as I was driving out of the parking lot, I saw that there was another vehicle coming straight for me in my lane. I assumed he hadn't seen me, so I tapped the horn lightly. He kept coming, so I hit it harder. By this point, I could see his face. He looked as if he was high on something, and I don't mean life. He slowed down a bit, but he still hit me head-on. I got out to check the damage (I know—big mistake).

He got out too, and I said to him, "There's not much damage here. I think I'm fine. Didn't you hear me?"

To which he replied, "Listen ——, if you don't want more trouble, you'd better get back in your —— car and get the —— out of here!"

I was shocked. I got back in the car, reversed, and then went around him, and when I thought I was at a safe distance, I pulled into a parking lot and cried and cried. I felt very intimidated, threatened, and really cross too. The exhaustion of the whole relocation was overwhelming and felt just too much for me.

We had sold most of our furniture in Nashville. We were moving from a traditional- to an Italian-style home, and our old stuff didn't fit. Unfortunately, the new stuff was going to take weeks to arrive. We were sleeping on mattresses on the floor, which was fine the first night, but I made a big discovery on the second night.

Demon Beast

I woke up and looked at the clock. It was three o'clock in the morning. I was thirsty, so I tiptoed to the kitchen to get some water. I knew I couldn't trip over anything as there was no furniture to trip over. I was almost there when I felt something on my foot. When I looked down and by the light of the moon shining through the windows, I saw that I had a scorpion on my left foot. Yes, a scorpion! I screamed and threw my leg up in the air. Barry and Christian came running out to see what was wrong.

"There is a demon beast on my foot! It has a forked tail, and I think its eyes were glowing."

Barry switched the lights on and revealed a small brown scorpion on the floor.

"It's not a demon beast; it's a scorpion," he said.

"Well, I'm not sleeping on the floor in a house infested with killer beasts."

That night, I slept in the middle of a pile of all our mattresses with Barry on one side, Christian on the other, and Belle on guard at my head. The next day, the bug man came, and I asked him to get his big guns out and spray the house and the yard until an elephant on steroids couldn't survive.

Just Give Me the Pills!

Things began to settle down. I avoided that particular Starbucks, and no more woman-eating critters appeared. One morning, as I took my anti-depression medication, I realized that I was almost out and didn't have any refills left. I see a psychiatrist twice a year and still take medication for depression every day. Now I was going to have to find a new shrink.

I had already found a new pediatrician, new gynecologist, new general practitioner, new dentist, and new hairstylist. The thought of having to start all over again with a fresh psychiatrist and give them my whole history was daunting. Psychiatrists write while you are talking, even if you are just talking about the weather. If you cough, they record it: "Was it an angry cough?"

Then I remembered that Dr. Paul Meier had an out-patient clinic in Dallas. I had interviewed Paul a couple of times on *The 700 Club*. I liked him; he always came across as kind and compassionate. I called his assistant to see if he would be willing to see me, and she said that he would.

It was lovely to see him again, and as I sat down he said, "I don't do counseling anymore. I can just do your meds."

I said, "That's great. I don't need a chat; the pills will be fine."

We caught up on each other's news as he wrote a few details about goodness-knows-what on my chart. Then the shrink in him kicked in, and despite his previous disclaimer, he began to ask some questions about my childhood. I filled him in as best I could, and then he hit a raw nerve.

I Don't Understand

He asked me about the times when my father would become very angry. "When your father felt that uncontrollable rage coming on, did he take it out on all three children?"

I sat for a few moments and didn't say anything. For most of my life, I have carried this wound in the depth of my closet, in the darkest spot available. It has never made sense to me that Dad took his anger out only on me, not my sister or brother. It's not that I wanted that to happen. I adore my brother and sister; it's just that I thought Dad and I were close.

I said to Dr. Meier, "It really hurts to think that when my dad wasn't able to control what he was doing, what he really felt came out."

He replied, "It did, Sheila, but not in the way you think."

The Gift

Dr. Meier explained to me that when part of the brain is destroyed, and the person suffering doesn't know what to do with what is going on inside, he hits out at the one person that he believes will still love him, no matter what.

"Your dad wasn't telling you that he didn't love you; he was telling you in the only way he could how much he did."

I wouldn't take a million dollars for that moment. It was as if in a split second God reached down into the darkest place in my life and held out His hand for me to come with Him. All the years of feeling ashamed and afraid seemed to melt away, and I stood up taller and lifted up my head. As I left Dr. Meier's office that day, I found myself whispering, "I understand now, Dad, I understand."

Light in the Darkest Places

I have shared this story publicly and have seen flashes of recognition from other women who experienced childhood pain through a parent who struggled with brain damage or mental illness. I also have encountered a troubling response from women in abusive relationships who take a different message from my story. One woman said to me, "Do you think that when my husband hits me, it is his way of telling me that he really loves me?" My answer to that is a resounding no! If you are in a situation like this, I urge you to find help and would remind you how God's Word describes love:

> Love is patient and kind. Love is not jealous, it does not brag, and it is not proud. Love is not rude, is not selfish, and does not get upset with others. Love does not count up wrongs that have been done. Love takes no pleasure in evil but rejoices over the truth. Love patiently accepts all things. It always trusts, always hopes, and always endures. —1 Corinthians 13:4–7 (NCV)

No Quick Fixes

The brain is such a complicated instrument. It only accounts for about 2 percent of our body weight but affects who we are and how we live. Like a computer, it records information and saves it to the hard drive of our soul. Computers are wonderful and maddening at the same time. When mine works well, I find myself wondering how I ever lived without it, but when it freezes or malfunctions, it becomes the enemy in my midst. I uncovered a little trick recently that has helped me fix small problems. I discovered that I can tell my computer to go back to the settings I had at an earlier date and it will restore those original settings.

If the problem is much greater, I can take it back to the original factory settings, and when I turn it on, it's as if I just bought it.

Wouldn't it be wonderful if we could do that with our lives? If we could erase any bad memory and restore original factory settings? We don't get to clean our hard drive, as it were, but we are invited to bring the broken pieces to the One who made us, and He will give us the grace to live with understanding and hope again.

A New Beginning

When we left Adam and Eve, they were standing before God in the pathetic garments that they tried to assemble from leaves. Even in His anger, God remembered mercy, and He made outfits for them from the skins of animals.

The tree of life remained in the Garden, and had they been able to eat from it, they would never have aged. Now they would face what you and I face every day, telltale grey hairs, little lines around the eyes, and the aches and pains of aging joints.

God's Word promises us that we will see that tree again one day:

> Then the angel showed me the river of the water of life. It was shining like crystal and was flowing from the throne of God and of the Lamb down the middle of the street of the city. The tree of life was on each side of the river. It produces fruit twelve times a year, once each month. The leaves of the tree are for the healing of all the nations. —Revelation 22:1–2 (NCV)

God didn't destroy the tree, but rather He set cherubim to guard it with a flaming sword that turned in every direction. One day, God will invite us to eat of that tree again, and all memory of the

Fall will be gone. But for now, we, like Adam and Eve, must carry on the business of living.

What About Us?

Within the church, two camps for dealing with painful memories seem to exist: those who encourage counseling and therapy, and those who believe that all a Christian has to remember is that she is a new creature in Christ, old things are passed away, and God has made everything new. There are extremes in these camps too. I have talked with many women who believe that because of the trauma of past events, they will never be free of pain and able to live a whole life again. They remain caught in the tornado of one event and are forever spinning, revisiting the circumstances over and over again. On the other side, there are those who believe that it is unacceptable for Christians to receive counseling from anyone other than their pastor, and medication of any kind for mental illness is sinful.

I have set up my own little camp in the middle of those two extremes. I have found a nice spot by fresh running water, and I would love for you to join me.

> He lets me rest in green pastures.
> He leads me to calm water.
> He gives me new strength.
> He leads me on paths that are right
> for the good of his name.
> Even if I walk through a very dark valley,
> I will not be afraid,
> because you are with me.
> Your rod and your shepherd's staff comfort me.
> —Psalm 23:2–4 (NCV)

The Loaves and Fishes Principle Revisited

If we choose to remain locked in our pain, we are unable to help anyone else. If we refuse to face it and stuff it back into the depths of our closet, pretend we are just fine, and don our cape and boots again, we are unable to relate to anyone else. I marvel at the way our Father redeems our pain. When we are able to face what has happened and bring it into the light and allow the risen Christ to meet us there, miracles can happen.

God deals with us all as individuals, so I trust the Holy Spirit to give you wisdom to know what you should do. If you feel that you are stuck and don't know how to work through what you are dealing with, I recommend talking with a counselor, pastor, or a woman whom you respect, and getting some help. There are several good information sources to help with choosing a counselor. 1–800–NEW–LIFE keeps a registry of reputable therapists, as does Meier Clinics at 1–888–7CLINIC. You can check out several helpful links at my Web site, www.sheilawalsh.com.

Our Pain Redeemed

I think that the enemy of our souls would love us to either remain in our pain with no ray of hope or cover it over even though it is affecting how we live our lives. When we are able by God's grace to give the broken pieces to the Lord, the loaves and fishes of our story, then Jesus will bless it, break it, and feed His people. Our lives will then be a lifeline to others who are coming behind us. We will be amazed at what God can do when we are willing to let Him.

A Look in the Mirror

How have you dealt with pain in your past?

Can you see ways that God can redeem the worst moments of your life?

Are you willing to allow God to open a door for you out of your pain?

A Closet Prayer

Father,

I thank You that even though I live in a broken world, You are always with me. I invite You by Your Holy Spirit to open a door for me and show me the way to go. I want You to use my life to bring hope to others.

For Jesus' sake,
Amen.

Twelve

Returning What Doesn't Fit:

I won't take on other people's dreams or offenses

*When He had called the multitude to Himself, He said to them,
"Hear and understand:*
  *"Not what goes into the mouth defiles a man; but what
comes out of the mouth, this defiles a man."*
  *Then His disciples came and said to Him, "Do you know
that the Pharisees were offended when they heard this saying?"*

—MATTHEW 15:10–12 (NKJV)

*An ill-fitting dress
Color, style, the fabric and more
Time to take it back*

—SHEILA WALSH

I will always think of it as the movie with the Paris buns. Mom took
my sister, Frances, and me on the train to Glasgow to see *The Sound
of Music.* Before we went in, we purchased a bag of large, sugar-
coated pastries at the bakery. I don't know whether we thought it
was going to be a particularly long movie or if we wanted ballast to
weigh us down in case the music and scenery were so breathtaking
we might float away!

I can still see the three of us sitting in the balcony, plowing into these monstrous creations. When the movie began, I put mine back in the bag and allowed myself to be transported to Austria. When Maria burst into "The hills are alive," I almost shouted, "Hallelujah," but I was too full.

If you have seen the movie, you will remember the story. If you haven't, I highly recommend renting it. In brief, Maria, a novice in a strict Salzburg abbey, loves the majestic landscape of the Alps and often forgets about prayer and all the other duties of a nun. She wants to stay out on "her hills" all day. Sister Margaretta is sympathetic to the young novice, but Sister Bertha has little patience for Maria and calls her a demon!

> "She'd outpester any pest
> Drive a hornet from its nest."[1]

The Mother Abbess, a very wise woman, thinks Maria might have mistaken her calling. It's clear to her that she is better suited to life outside the convent. She sends Maria to Captain von Trapp's villa to act as a governess for his seven children who have lost their mother.

There Maria finds her passion as she cares for the children who are living under the strict military code of their father, and she finds the love of her life in Captain von Trapp. The wedding scene in the grand cathedral is one of the most beautiful moments in the movie— it even made my sister put her bun down, and that's not easy to do! The nuns are able to watch the ceremony, and even Sister Bertha has a tear in her eye.

It is a wonderful thing to see someone find the path that is right for her. It can even make the most cynical and embittered rejoice if only for a moment.

The Freedom of the Cross

The movie is based on the true story of George and Maria von Trapp. They fled Nazi-occupied Austria instead of cooperating with Hitler's régime that eventually led to World War II. Rosemaria von Trapp, one of the real-life children, had this to say about her famous parents in an interview in 1994:

> Only yesterday, I talked to high school students—sophomores—who were doing research papers on the Holocaust of Hitler in Germany. They wanted me to talk about the Nazis. I told them that Hitler gave us a symbol of a cross with hooks on it. But our Christian faith gives us a symbol of a cross that brings freedom and resurrection. The world, you know, offers us a glossy cross with hooks in it. My father and mother had to make a choice. They chose the cross of Christ.[2]

I love the simple statement: "our Christian faith gives us a symbol of a cross that brings freedom and resurrection."

Part of the freedom we have in Christ is finding out what He has called us to and giving our whole hearts to it. When I stand on the platform at Women of Faith and look out at a crowd of fifteen to twenty thousand women, many questions are in my mind and silent prayers in my heart. *How many are covering up the pain in their lives? How many came in wearing an overcoat of shame, grateful that the lights are down so that they can remain anonymous in the crowd? How many are living the life they imagined, and how many are struggling with how their lives turned out? How many in this room feel truly free? Father, show us what it means to be fearfully and wonderfully made. Why is it so hard to see ourselves as You see us?*

As you reflect on your own life, do you feel free? Does it seem to you that even though life can be hard at times, you are enjoying the freedom and grace that comes from carrying the burden perfectly designed for you? Or do you feel that the weight you pick up every day is too heavy and ill-fitting? The ill-designed burdens we carry can be those we have imposed on ourselves or those that others have asked us to carry.

Part of the process of cleaning out my Wonder Woman closet was recognizing how much I was carrying on my shoulders that Jesus never asked me to pick up. Rather than being like a child delighting in the unconditional love of her Father, I was like Thomas O'Malley, our stray cat.

Would You Like Fries with that Mouse?

One night when I was taking out the trash, I heard a rustle in a bush. I looked over and saw a silver head and two dark eyes staring back at me. I called to this mystery kitty, but it ran away. Every night after that, I would peek out, and there he would be. He would always run if I came too close, so I began my campaign to win him over.

I began with some tuna fish in a saucer. I put it near the bush, and then I moved out of the way and sat on the grass. He approached it cautiously, never taking his eyes off me. Every night after that, I moved a little closer. Two weeks later, once he had eaten, he came over to me and let me scratch his head.

Christian named him Thomas O'Malley after the alley cat in the Disney movie *The Aristocats*. We became fast friends. He wouldn't come in the house, but when I sat on the patio at the back of our house, he would jump up on my chair and sit on my lap.

One day, Christian raced into the kitchen to tell me something was wrong with Thomas. He was laying on our back step with a huge gash down his back that was bleeding profusely. I knew he needed stitches, but I didn't know how he would respond to being picked up and put in my car. I got a towel and knelt beside him. "Thomas, I need to get help for you. I know you are afraid, but you can trust me. I will take care of you." (Yes, I speak Cat!)

I wrapped the towel around him, and Barry gently lifted him into the car. The vet kept him in for a few days until his deep wound began to heal. When I went to bring him home, I had no idea how he would feel about me now. How could a cat understand that this ordeal that he had been put through was for his own good? I was sure that to Thomas I was now assigned the role of the beast who took him to a place of torture. I was not prepared for his grateful response.

From that day until the day he died, Thomas became the consummate gift-giver. Each morning when I would open the back door to give him some milk, there would be some decapitated offering on the mat, part of a mouse or bird. Occasionally, I would get the head, too, as a special treat. There was no way to tell him that a simple purr would have been fine.

For much of my life, I was like Thomas in my relationship with God. Every morning I would drag my latest "gift" to Him. It would be one more thing that I was going to do for Him, or one more prayer group I was going to join, one more person to help, or one more task to undertake. I meet women like this every weekend, but one in particular stands out.

I Hate This!

I saw her leaning up against the wall, watching me as I signed books. I wondered at first if she wasn't feeling well. Then I saw a tear begin to run down her cheek. I never get to talk with everyone that I would like to at our events, but every now and then, I feel

God prompt me to approach someone who might not come close to me. I excused myself from my book line, walked over to her, and asked her if there was anything I could do.

She said, "I'm watching you signing books and listening to everyone and taking time with each woman, and it makes me feel like such a hypocrite."

I asked her why she felt that way.

"I'm head of the women's ministry at my church," she replied. "I volunteered to take over when our pastor and his wife left. I hate it."

"Why don't you step down?" I asked.

"What would people think of me?" she said, her tone betraying shock at the thought.

"Does that matter?" I asked.

"Of course, it matters! What kind of witness would I be if I quit?"

"Do you believe that God called you to fill this position?" I asked.

"I don't really know, but I said I would do it, and people are counting on me."

"And you're miserable," I said.

"Yes," she whispered, "I'm miserable."

Worn-Out

Can you relate to that? Are you the woman that everyone else counts on to be there because you always have in the past? Are you the one who is overworked and underpaid, but you smile, saying that you're doing it all for Jesus even though you are silently muttering in your heart?

What I told that woman that day was that I have been there too. I have been the smiling face and willing hands that mask a worn-out, disillusioned, weary soul. When you are in that place, there is no real joy; everything feels like an effort, an ill-fitting burden. So even if those around you see you as a wonderful woman who serves God with everything she has, you know the sad truth: under the cape, you are just plain worn-out. Like the Wizard of Oz, one day, I was caught with my cape off.

Another Bad Wizard Moment

It was after five o'clock, and I was hurrying to get out of my office at the Christian Broadcasting Network. I had people coming over for dinner later, and I still had a lot to do. As I pulled my office door shut, my secretary put her hand over the telephone receiver and said to me, "I think this girl really needs to talk to you." Patricia was sensitive to the demands of two live daily television shows (as well as *The 700 Club,* I had my own show called *Heart to Heart*) and knew that I couldn't possibly speak to everyone who called, so when she sensed I should take a call, I trusted her judgment.

I asked her to transfer it downstairs to my dressing room so that I could change while I talked. I picked up the receiver and began to listen as the girl shared her story. After about five minutes, she said, "If you didn't want to take my call, why didn't you just say so?"

I was shocked. "What do you mean?" I asked.

"You sound so impatient, as if you are in a hurry. I can hardly finish a sentence before you want to give me a quick fix."

Caught! Exposed! A very bad Wizard!

"I am so sorry," I said. "You're right, and I'm wrong, and I'm so sorry."

We talked for a while, and she graciously forgave me. When I got off the phone, I wept. As I reflect on that moment now, I had two good, perfectly acceptable choices. I could have said to Patricia, "I'm sorry, Pat, I need to go; will you put her through to one of our counselors?" Or I could have got down on my knees and said,

"Father, in my own strength, I don't have anything left to give to this girl, so I ask You to fill me with Your love and grace in Jesus' name."

I didn't do either. I didn't want to appear as if I didn't care, but I didn't take the time to ask God to help me. I thought I could keep to my own little schedule and fit her in as I went. She pulled back the curtain just as Toto did and exposed the truth. Jesus gladly welcomes failed wizards and makes us into real people. He takes us when we are at the end of ourselves, our own efforts, when we no longer know who we are, and teaches us how to live again.

> "Are you tired? Worn out? Burned out on religion? Come to me. Get away with me and you'll recover your life. I'll show you how to take a real rest. Walk with me and work with me—watch how I do it. Learn the unforced rhythms of grace. I won't lay anything heavy or ill-fitting on you."
> —Matthew 11:28–29 (The Message)

I wonder what percentage of God's family is wearing ill-fitting garments. Sometimes the weight we carry is not a burden we took up for ourselves to please God or others but one we took up as an offense for someone else.

I Don't Trust Them Anymore

I was taking calls on a radio interview one day when one caller's opening sentence took me by surprise: "Just think of me as hostile."

As we talked back and forth, her opening statement was accurate. As far as she was concerned, there was not a trustworthy believer in the body of Christ. I asked her what had happened to hurt her so deeply and discovered that it was not her own offense but an offense she had witnessed against her mother.

As a young girl, she had watched her mom receive mistreatment by a few women in church. Though it must have wounded the mom, it had branded the daughter. I asked if her mother had stopped attending church. She said that her mom was still very involved; she had been able to forgive and move on. It was the daughter who was stuck and would not let go.

I understand this. It is much harder to watch someone we love being hurt than to be hurt ourselves. Just ask many pastors' wives who watch their husbands come home from elders' meetings or church meetings with barbs in their hearts. It is easy to become bitter, but it is deadly. I asked this woman if she would meet with me the next time I was in her city, and she said she would.

In my own efforts, there is nothing I can do or say that can change a thing. It is my prayer that God who knows her heart and her pain will take the loaves and fishes of my life and feed this dried-up heart. Life is too precious to waste it by holding onto a grudge, no matter how justified. I saw this woman as a bird trapped in a cage, madly beating her wings against the bars.

Skandallon

One of the translations for *offense* is "skandallon." The word *skandallon* is Greek and describes a trap or device used to catch birds and small animals. Jesus used this word when he said to Peter, "Get behind Me, Satan! You are an offense to Me, for you are not mindful of the things of God, but the things of men" (Matt. 16:23 NKJV).

Christ sensed that, through Peter, Satan was trying to trap him. It is important to recognize where offense comes from, and who stands just behind it, longing to catch us in its snare.

I feel such a sense of urgency in my spirit as I write this. Offense is one of the enemy's most potent tools. It has devastated many believers and kept them in bondage all their lives. As you reflect on your own heart, is there offense rooted there? It is important to understand that even if you are right, even if there is justifiable cause for your feelings, if you let them take root and dig deep into your heart, you have given the enemy a place to live. No matter how long you nurse a grudge, it won't get better.

Are You Offended by God?

At times we are offended with God because we don't understand what He is doing. After the Passover meal, "Jesus told his followers, 'Tonight you will all stumble in your faith on account of me, because it is written in the Scriptures: "I will kill the shepherd, and the sheep will scatter" (Matt. 26:31 NCV). Jesus uses the word *skandallon* here as he tells the disciples that God's plan will be so offensive to Christ's followers, they will scatter like sheep.

God knows that we do not always understand His ways and thoughts. It is time to take our offenses, the roots of bitterness against Him or against others, to Jesus and let Him set us free. It is time to take our ill-fitting garments out of the closet and lay them at the foot of the Cross.

A Look in the Mirror

As you look at your life, what areas feel like a burden to you?

How much of what you are doing is in God's strength and how much are you battling alone?

Are you offended by God Himself?

Where are the roots of offense in your life?

Are you willing to let them go?

A Closet Prayer

Dear Father,

I am tired of trying to be Wonder Woman. I am also afraid to drop the cape and let myself be seen in my humanity. I ask You to help me. Please show me where I have allowed offense to take root, and give me the grace to bring those offenses to You.

For Jesus' sake,
Amen.

Thirteen

Altering My View:

I will change the way I see myself

"Look, here comes another brood, as if there were not enough of us already! And what a queer looking object one of them is; we don't want him here," and then one flew out and bit him in the neck.

"Let him alone," said the mother; "he is not doing any harm."

"Yes, but he is so big and ugly," said the spiteful duck, "and therefore he must be turned out."[1]

—HANS CHRISTIAN ANDERSEN, *THE UGLY DUCKLING*

But Jesus said, "Someone did touch me, because I felt power go out from me." When the woman saw she could not hide, she came forward, shaking, and fell down before Jesus. While all the people listened, she told why she had touched him and how she had been instantly healed.

—LUKE 8:46–47 (NCV)

When God created Adam and Eve, they were perfect swans, beautiful and strong. There was no concept of an ugly duckling. He named them both Adam, and there was equality and grace in their role and stature before God—then everything changed.

When they looked into each other's eyes, they saw a new reflection. It was unappealing and . . . wrong. It changed the way they saw each other. For the first time, they experienced distance, separateness. As they saw each other differently, it changed the way they related to each other.

What Might Have Been

If we had been born into Eden, things would have been so different. Let me highlight a few things that you would have enjoyed as one of God's perfect swans: You would have looked at your reflection and loved it. You would never have asked, "How do I look in this?" because you would have known you were beautiful. You would have looked at every other woman in a room and praised God for her beauty and grace.

Can you imagine what that would be like? One day, we will enjoy that again, but for now, we live in a very different place. We live in a world and in a culture that constantly highlights for women where we fall short; where our feathers are all stubby and brown.

I picked up a copy of a well-known fashion magazine the other day when my flight was delayed. As I flipped through the pages detailing the fashion for the coming season, I saw models who were 6 feet tall and a size 2. They were wearing things that in my wildest imagination I couldn't come up with. They looked like exotic, colorful, fragile birds.

Couture, or high-end fashion, impacts what is sold in every store. So whether you shop at Neiman Marcus or Target, the fashion gurus of Paris, Milan, and New York attempt to dress each one of us. My heart is most troubled for the little ducklings in our midst.

I realize that I am now about to start sounding like my mother sounded to me when I was sixteen, but I am distressed by the clothes that some parents let their daughters wear. Walk through any mall, and you will see girls as young as ten and eleven in outfits that show off their stomachs and barely cover their bottoms. To me, this is not a fashion or generational thing; it is a sign of the times, of how far we have fallen from our swan-like state.

When I was sixteen, I wore some goofy things. I was part of the Jesus Movement inspired by many of the contemporary Christian artists. We wore ratty jeans and vivid t-shirts, and my pride and joy was my afghan coat. I have no idea what animal it came from, but when it got wet, it smelled like a dead afghan hound.

But the clothes that are being foisted onto our young girls are so far away from the garments of Eden; they are the garments of the Fall. It breaks my heart to see what has become of us.

Yellow Polka-Dot Bikini

In February of 2005, Women of Faith held its national conference in Las Vegas, Nevada. We asked our hotel booker if we could be in a hotel off the main strip in Vegas, hoping that it would be more family-oriented than the big casinos. Barry, Christian, Mary (his nanny in 2005), and I checked in, and as we were waiting in the lobby, Christian said to me, "Mom, look at that girl." I turned to see a show girl dancing on a table just six feet away from us in what can only be described as three very small handkerchiefs. "Why do you think she's dressed like that?" he asked.

"It's very hot," I replied in a weak, pathetic voice.

It was all downhill from that point. Vegas has walked away from its attempt to be a more family-friendly place and returned to its roots as Sin City. The phrase touted everywhere is "What happens in Vegas, stays in Vegas." In other words, you can do what you like here, and no one will ever find out. The remnant of Christians in Vegas have come up with their own motto, "What happens in Vegas, changes the world." That's why we were there, to partner with them in their desire to bring the fragrance of Christ to the dark stench of life without Him. Vegas seemed to be the perfect city to bring a message of hope and healing to: "But where sin abounded, grace abounded much more" (Rom. 5:20 NKJV). We had an amazing conference. Eight hundred and forty-seven women made commitments to Christ.

As we were boarding the plane to fly home, Christian looked at me and said, "If I never see another bikini as long as I live, that's fine with me!" He's only eight years old! Aaargh!!!

Las Vegas is an extreme exhibition of how far we have fallen, but the signs are there in every town and village across our land. Just as the external landscape has changed since Eden, so has our internal landscape.

There Once Was an Ugly Duckling

Eve is the only woman to have known what it feels like to be a perfectly beautiful swan. What a rude awakening it must have been after the Fall for her to see her reflection in the water and discover how it had changed. Just as the other ducks rejected the ugly duckling, we have experienced moments like that. Rejection takes many forms. It can come from the look we see in the eyes of someone else, or it can come from our own hearts as we gaze at our reflection.

From Eden to Edenhall

I spent most of my childhood and all my teenage years at 8 Edenhall Road, Ayr, Scotland. We lived in a small, semidetached rented house. Stephen had his own room, and Frances and I shared. It was within those four walls that I shed many tears, despising the image I saw in the mirror.

When I was fifteen years old, a ballet troop visited our school and performed some modern pieces. One of the girls was exactly how I wished I could be. She was very slim and probably a size 32B bra while I was not thin and a size 36D. She had skin that seemed to glow and perfect white teeth. My skin was more like a page out of *War and Peace* in braille, and my teeth reflected my fifteen cups of tea a day. I hated what I saw in the mirror. I used to save my allowance in a box under the bed so that when I was older I could have plastic surgery and be what I thought would be the perfect bra size.

I know now that there is no such thing as perfection on this earth, but as a young girl I saw in others all that I wished I could be. I saw how the boys reacted when one of the pretty girls came into a room. I stood awkwardly in gym class as boys chose practice partners for our senior dance, knowing that I would be one of the last chosen.

As I have said, I turn fifty in the summer of 2006. I like my reflection in the mirror now. I am one of those women who looked better at forty than she did at twenty, but every weekend I see young women in my book-signing line, and I recognize myself. I see the unsure half smile, and I hear the silent cry behind their eyes longing to be accepted and loved but braced for rejection. I want to tell each one of them: what changed my life wasn't losing some weight or having my skin clear up; it was touching the hem of Jesus' garment.

Desperate Enough

During the 2005 conference year, our dramatist, Nicole Johnson, presented a sketch on a woman we read about in Mark and Luke's gospels. She is known as the woman "who had been bleeding for twelve years" (Luke 8:43 NCV). Nicole's poignant work inspired me to look at this woman and imagine what life must have been like for her:

A woman was in the crowd who had been bleeding for twelve years, but no one was able to heal her. She came up behind Jesus and touched the edge of his coat, and instantly her bleeding stopped. Then Jesus said, "Who touched me?"

When all the people said they had not touched him, Peter said, "Master, the people are all around you and are pushing against you."

But Jesus said, "Someone did touch me, because I felt power go out from me." When the woman saw she could not hide, she came forward, shaking, and fell down before Jesus. While all the people listened, she told why she had touched him and how she had been instantly healed. Jesus said to her, "Dear woman, you are made well because you believed. Go in peace."
—Luke 8:43–48 (NCV)

A Despised Gender

The rabbis of Jesus's day had little time or use for women. Their attitude can be seen in writings recorded during the two centuries after Jesus.

"Talk not much with womankind." (Yose b. Yohanan of Jerusalem, quoted from *mAbot* 1.5)

"Do not speak excessively with a woman lest this ultimately lead you to adultery." (The Talmud, quoted from *bNed.201*)

"A man should not speak with a woman in the market, even if she is his wife, much less another woman, because the public may misinterpret it." (*Abot de Rabbi Nathan*, quoted from ARNA 2, p.9)

"We have not found that the Almighty spoke to a woman except Sarah." (R. Eliezer b. R. Shimeon, quoted from *ySot.7.1,2lb*)

In light of these writings, Jesus' treatment of women becomes even more remarkable. His tender interaction with women of all social classes violates the Pharisaical rules[2] and begins the redemption promised in the Garden of Eden, lifting women out of a very secondary place and restoring dignity and worth. When Jesus met the woman who had been hemorrhaging for twelve years, He clearly revealed, to all who were there and all who would read her story down through the centuries, His heart for women.

Jesus encountered this woman while He was on his way to Jairus's house. Jairus was an important man, one of the rulers in the synagogue in Capernaum, whose twelve-year-old daughter, his only daughter, was dying. He found Jesus, fell at His feet, and begged Him to come and heal his precious girl. Jesus agreed to go with him, but as they were walking toward his house, this woman in the crowd reached out and touched the edge of Jesus' robe. She did the unthinkable, broke several "rules," and yet she received an absolute miracle.

Unclean

Those around her considered this woman *niddah*. This is a Jewish word meaning "unclean." Rules about how a woman should behave when she was menstruating were strict and specific. Regulations about how a man should be with his wife when she was having her period were also very strict. Men were taught by the rabbis that they should stay away from their wives for several days before and after her menstrual flow. They used a verse in Leviticus to support this: "So you must warn the people of Israel to stay separated from things that make them unclean. If you don't warn the people, they might make my Holy Tent unclean, and then they would have to die!" (Lev. 15:31 NCV)

Many rabbis taught that if a man had any kind of contact with his wife during the seven or eight days after the end of her period, he might die. Rabbi Yoshayah wrote of a woman whose husband, a prominent teacher, had died suddenly while a young man. He asked her how her husband behaved in the days just following her cycle:

> "He ate with me, drank with me, and slept with me in bodily contact, and it did not occur to him to engage in sex."
> I said to her: "Blessed be the Omnipresent for slaying him!"[3]

If you calculate the days before a woman's period, the days her period occurs, and the days following her period as days when her husband couldn't come near her, it's a wonder God's people survived at all!

But this woman in question was in a desperate state. She had been bleeding for twelve years. She had spent everything she had trying to find a cure and nothing had helped. She was virtually an outcast. No one would invite her to sit on their furniture or eat off their regular dishes, as everything she touched would become unclean as well. Can you imagine how miserable and desperate her life must have been? She was desperate enough to risk everything to touch Jesus.

Luke indicates that there was a crowd around Jesus as He made His way to Jairus's house when suddenly He stopped and asked an unusual question, "Who touched Me?"

The disciples didn't understand the question as the crowd had been pressing in on them all day. But Jesus wasn't asking them; He was giving this woman who risked everything an opportunity for a face-to-face encounter with the Lamb of God. Jesus knew that something had happened to her; He felt it. He felt the power of God go out of Him.

She could have walked away unseen. She knew she was healed. Wasn't that enough? Wasn't that what she had come for? But Jesus asked her if she wanted more. He gave her an opportunity to tell her story out loud. Most of us dread that. We would rather God just heal us quietly somewhere, and we can slip away unnoticed, but there is more if we want it.

We read that she came out of the crowd and fell at Jesus' feet. Before Him and the crowd of whispering onlookers, she told her story. Wow! There is such freedom in telling your story out loud. You discover that you don't self-combust, the sun is still in the sky, and, best of all, you get to hear Jesus say, "Daughter, your faith has made you well; go in peace" (Luke 8:48 NRSV).

If she had slipped away that day, what would she have missed? She would have missed the beautiful greeting, "Daughter." She would have missed Christ honoring her faith and desperation. She would have missed Christ's benediction to go in peace, and she would have missed looking into the eyes of the Lamb of God who takes away the sin of the world.

What Jesus did that day was remarkable. He transformed the life of a woman who had no life. He took someone who was desperate, who saw herself as unclean, unlovable, and unrecognized, and He restored health, dignity, and grace. Her faith moved Him, and even though He was on the way to the house of a wealthy, respected man, He stopped for the silent cry of a poor, hopeless woman.

I don't know what you see when you look in your mirror. Perhaps you see someone who doesn't belong, an ugly duckling inside or out who has no hope of being set free. I invite you to do what I did in 1992 when I felt most unattractive and desperate; I reached out and touched the hem of Jesus' garment. When Jesus stopped and asked, "Who touched me?" I said, "I did." I've been telling about it ever since.

She, too, who touched Thee in the press
And healing virtue stole,
Was answered, "Daughter, go in peace;
Thy faith has made thee whole."
. . . Like her, with hopes and fears we come
To touch Thee if we may;
O send us not despairing home;
Send none unhealed away.[4]

A Look in the Mirror

If you were asked to describe yourself, what words would you use?

When you look in a mirror, what do you see reflected back at you?

Where are the places in your heart and soul that bleed?

Are you willing to reach out to Jesus and touch Him?

A Closet Prayer

Father God,

When I look in my mirror, I see so many things that are wrong. I see ugliness outside, and I carry woundedness inside. I ask You to give me the grace and strength to reach out and touch the edge of Jesus' garment.

In His name,
Amen.

Getting Help:

I will allow others to bring healing to my life

Just then, some men were carrying on a mat a man who was paralyzed. They tried to bring him in and put him down before Jesus. But because there were so many people there, they could not find a way in. So they went up on the roof and lowered the man on his mat through the ceiling into the middle of the crowd right before Jesus. Seeing their faith, Jesus said, "Friend, your sins are forgiven."

—LUKE 5:18–20 (NCV)

Help me get my feet back on the ground, won't you please, please help me?

—JOHN LENNON AND PAUL MCCARTNEY, "HELP" (1965)

Christian and I call her "Poor Ruth." The title confused her at first. She makes a good income as an interior designer, so it couldn't refer to her economic status. Her feet bother her a bit, but other than that, she's in good shape, physically. Christian explained our choice of title one day as she and Barry were heading out our front door to go shopping for rugs: "Miss Ruth, Mom and I call you 'Poor

Ruth' because we know what it's like to go shopping with Dad. He's very . . . picky."

"A perfectionist," I added.

"Driven," Christian threw in.

"Obsessed even," I suggested.

Ruth smiled and said, "Oh, I've handled worse than your father," and with a naïve smile, she was gone.

We closed the door and looked at one another and said, "Poor Ruth."

The Perfect Rugs

They returned several hours later. Christian and I were waiting at the front door. We escorted Ruth to the sofa. Christian helped her take off her shoes, and I put her legs up on a footstool. She looked at us with a glazed desperation.

"I know, Ruth," I said. "Don't try to talk!"

Five rugs—how hard could that be?

Barry has a gift for decorating, even if those who assist him require extensive therapy afterward. Our new home has travertine floors and hardwood, so we needed rugs to warm the rooms up. Poor Ruth told Barry that she had the perfect contact for nice rugs that wouldn't break the bank. When she staggered back into the house that day, I asked Barry if they had found what they were looking for. He told me that the store was amazing, but he disagreed with the suggestion of the senior sales associate.

"I showed her pictures of the house and some of our furniture. She told me that we need deep navy and red rugs for our style of home, but I told her that we want black and red," he said.

"We do?" I said.

"We do," he replied with a confident smile.

Round One

The first round of rugs arrived. There was one for the dining room, the living room, the den, my office, and a round rug for the entrance way. I thought they were lovely, but I was wrong! Barry said that they were too black and needed to have more red.

Round Two

As I watched the men unfurl the rugs, I was sure these had to be right: more red and less black. Oh, foolish Galatian! Apparently the red was in the wrong place. You can have more red, but it can't be in just any old place.

Round Three

As I opened the door to let the two men in from the rug store, we exchanged vocal glances: theirs said, *I beg you—like these!* Mine said, *If only it were that simple.*

I will spare you rounds four, five, six, and seven. By round eight, I had taken to hiding behind a tree in the backyard when the rugs arrived. On the evening of round eight, I asked Barry what the real issue was.

"The colors seem wrong," he said. "It's as if the black doesn't tone in with everything else."

"Do you remember that originally the rug lady suggested that dark blue might work better?" I asked.

"I still think that's wrong," he said as he pulled out a magazine on Italian design. "If you look at all the rugs in here they are . . . they are . . . actually they are . . . blue."

A Winning Round

Round nine was a winner. As the rugs were carefully placed, Poor Ruth sat down on the sofa, and I am sure I could hear her quietly humming the "Hallelujah Chorus"! The blue rugs appear to be here to stay—there's talk of even cutting the tags off, but I'm not holding my breath just yet.

I tease Barry about his meticulous search for just the right thing, but I know that it means a lot to him that our home should be a place of beauty and sanctuary. What he is learning in all of this great home adventure though is to let others help him. It can be hard to accept help from others if that's not how you are wired. Barry's favorite saying is "Daddy knows!" Usually he is right, too, which can be very annoying.

Last Christmas, Christian and I ordered pajamas for him with "Daddy Knows" embroidered on the jacket pocket. We meant it as a joke. He took it as a huge compliment!

Some won't accept help from others because they think they don't need it—it's a pride issue. Others won't accept help because they think they're not worth helping—almost a reverse-pride issue. The truth is, we all need help from time to time. When we are open to allowing someone else to bring perspective and help, overcoming years of frustration can become a doable job.

Spring Cleaning Help

I have read that the definition of *insanity* is "to keep doing the same thing over and over again, expecting a different result." I wonder how many of us would be declared insane under that classification! Many of us try to make changes in our lives with no success. We try over and over, only to find ourselves back where we started. We need the input and sound guidance of those who are gifted to help others.

In the body of Christ, we all have different gifts. God gives diverse talents and abilities to each one of us to be used to strengthen His family and direct others to Him. Paul writes to the church in Rome highlighting some of those gifts:

> Each one of us has a body with many parts, and these parts all have different uses. In the same way, we are many, but in Christ we are all one body. Each one is a part of that body, and each part belongs to all the other parts. We all have different gifts, each of which came because of the grace God gave us. The person who has the gift of prophecy should use that gift in agreement with the faith. Anyone who has the gift of serving should serve. Anyone who has the gift of teaching should teach. Whoever has the gift of encouraging others should encourage. Whoever has the gift of giving to others should give freely. Anyone who has the gift of being a leader should try hard when he leads. Whoever has the gift of showing mercy to others should do so with joy. —Romans 12:4–8 (NCV)

All About God

It is clear that the gifts have little to do with the recipient and everything to do with the Giver. Every gift comes by the grace of God and is equal in His sight. The trouble is, they are not usually equal in our sight. Some gifts have more curb appeal than others in our culture.

For example, in most churches, a teacher or a leader receives more respect or is considered to be more valuable than someone whose gift is encouragement. But if we claim to hold a proper understanding of Scripture, we must learn to relate to each other rightly. It takes great internal vigilance to avoid the mind-set and values of our culture and have the mind of Christ as we look at one another.

When we have a biblical understanding of gifting, we more easily accept help from others who have gifts of compassion, mercy, helps, or discernment. It's not a case of saying, "I'm not as important as so-and-so because I don't know what to do here, and they do." It is making peace with the different gifts and abilities that God has given to each of us, given to help each other.

It takes a certain amount of internal fortitude to be able to ask for help and perhaps even more to receive it. It's only as we are freed from the clutter in Wonder Woman's closet—the shame, fear, insecurity, and anger—that we reach a safe enough place to ask for help without dissolving in tears or rejecting the helper. So often we live such lonely lives, and we don't have to.

Help Me If You Can

One of the most humbling but liberating experiences in life is to ask for help in areas where we think we should be competent. Perhaps you didn't have a good mother, and you struggle in your parenting. It's hard to reach out to someone and say, "Will you teach me how to be a good mom?" We think it should be instinctive, but that's not always so. If you have never experienced healthy parenting yourself, what you have received (or failed to receive) has left you ill-equipped for all you want to give. As moms, we are very hard on ourselves. Every little mistake or emotional response haunts us. Even when we strive to get it right, we beat ourselves up when we miss the mark. I admire women who have the grace to say that they don't know how to *be*. I admire it because I have been there many times, and I know how hard it is to admit it.

What Does Normal Look Like?

I had to ask Marilyn Meberg, one of my fellow Women of Faith speakers, to teach me how to be a good friend. I had been a loner for so long that I didn't know what "normal" looked like in a growing friendship between two women. For many years, I had kept a privacy wall around my heart and I needed help to dismantle it. My need was exposed on a trip we took together.

She and I were flying to Las Vegas to do some promotional appearances and radio interviews for our very first conference there. Because Christian was only two years old and I had no idea what Vegas might be like, he and Barry stayed home. Little did I know that just six short years later, Christian would have his own definition of Vegas!

I love Marilyn's sense of humor and was looking forward to being with her. We had great fun on the radio interviews, and when they were finished, we went back to the hotel for some free hours before our event in a local church that evening. Marilyn asked me what I was going to do. I told her that I might go shopping, and she said that would be fun.

I dropped some things in my room and took off by myself. It never crossed my mind to ask Marilyn if we could go together. I like being alone, and I assumed that she would rather be by herself than with me. I thought that if I asked her to join me, I would put her in the difficult spot of wanting to say no but not wanting to hurt my feelings.

I was a very public person, but I found it much easier to have short-term encounters than deep friendships. I desperately wanted deep friendships, but I didn't know how to cultivate them.

Several months later, when Marilyn and I were having dinner before a movie, I realized for the first time that I had hurt her feelings. She told me that she had been looking forward to spending time getting to know me better, but when I went off by myself, she took that as a signal to give me space. I asked Marilyn to forgive me and help me learn the art of friendship. We are now very close, and I treasure the intimate times we share together. I could have missed those because I didn't want to make a mistake or make a fool of myself or admit that I needed help.

Once we ask for help, however, it's up to us whether we take it or not.

Stuck

She said that she would wait until I had finished signing books so that we could have a more private chat. I told her that as I never get through my entire line during each break, it might be best if we grabbed a few moments as I signed her program.

"I can't pray at our small group. I want to, but when the time comes, I just can't. I freeze up. I know I'll say the wrong thing," she said.

"Have you talked with any of your friends about this?" I asked.

"Yes, they tell me that there is no right thing, just speak from the heart."

"That's pretty sound advice," I said.

"I know, but I just can't do it."

"Well, you don't have to pray in your small group. God knows your heart," I reminded her.

"I know, but I want to."

"Can I ask you a question?"

"Yes."

"How long have you been talking about this issue?"

"Oh, for years," she replied.

Unstuck

To make significant changes in our lives, we have to be willing, willing to allow God to show us where we need help and willing to let go of how we have previously defined ourselves.

There comes a point when we have to cut off the labels and make a commitment to a new identity. It took Barry months to come to the place where he could say, "These rugs are staying." Several times he was tempted to bring back some of the old rugs again, just to make absolutely sure he liked his decision, but with the threat of bodily harm hanging over him, he finally cut off each label and placed the pads beneath them. Our home is a more beautiful place because of Poor Ruth, the Rug Lady, and Barry. Teamwork can produce wonderful results!

A Look in the Mirror

What areas in your life do you need help with?

Why is it hard for you to ask for help?

How does it make you feel when you admit you need help?

Are you willing?

Are you ready?

A Closet Prayer

Father God,

Thank You that You have made me part of Your family. I ask You to show me where I need help and give me the grace and humility to ask for it.

In Jesus' name,
Amen.

Fifteen

Receiving God's Outfits for Me:
A divine makeover

To be born in a duck's nest, in a farmyard, is of no consequence to a bird, if it is hatched from a swan's egg. He now felt glad at having suffered sorrow and trouble, because it enabled him to enjoy so much better all the pleasure and happiness around him.[1]

—HANS CHRISTIAN ANDERSEN, *THE UGLY DUCKLING*

Now we see a dim reflection, as if we were looking into a mirror, but then we shall see clearly. Now I know only a part, but then I will know fully, as God has known me.

—1 CORINTHIANS 13:12 (NCV)

Have you ever had one of those "Eureka!" moments when something that was foggy suddenly becomes crystal clear? Beth Moore, beloved Bible teacher and author, described a moment like that to our Women of Faith audience in 2004.

Beth is a strong, passionate woman who loves God with a fervor I have not witnessed very often. Even so, she struggled with the shadows of past sin, unable to fully receive the joy of forgiveness. She described for us what took place one morning while she was leading a women's retreat in Montreat, North Carolina.

She was sharing a cabin with her dear friend and mine, Jan Silvious. The evening had been rich with the sense of God's presence and grace, and one more time, Beth wrestled with the question of why God would use her when she felt so unworthy. Jan did all she could to remind Beth of what she knew was true, the gift of the love and forgiveness of God, but Beth still went to bed with a heavy heart.

When she woke the next morning and looked out the window, she saw a sight that she had never seen before as a Texas girl. During the night, a blanket of snow had fallen, covering the earth with a clean, white, sparkling bedspread. Beth looked out as the sun made the snowflakes seem to dance for joy, and she had her "Eureka!" moment. In that winter gift from God, Beth finally knew in the depth of her being that because of the covering of the blood of Jesus Christ, she was clean!

> The LORD says,
> "Come, let us talk about these things.
> Though your sins are like scarlet,
>   they can be as white as snow.
> Though your sins are deep red,
>   they can be white like wool. —Isaiah 1:18 (NCV)

Those moments can come when we are waiting for them, or they can take us by surprise.

Lessons at Sea

I had one of those moments somewhere between Bar Harbor, Maine, and Halifax, Nova Scotia, in the summer of 2005. Our Women of Faith cruise was taking us to various ports from Boston, Massachusetts, to Montreal, Canada. It was a lovely voyage. As I stood on deck early that first morning, watching the sunrise, I thought back on my times at sea. On each of the three cruises that we have hosted, I have learned something significant about God, about myself, and about others.

Robin Hood and the Merry Walshs

Previously, we had taken our women to the Caribbean and to Alaska. I am not a big fan of the Caribbean cruise routes. There is something that seems obscene to me about docking in a luxury ship at ports where local families struggle with such abject poverty.

On the last trip, Barry, Christian, and I caused utter confusion for the ship's crew. They are used to seeing people get off the ship in a port with just a small bag and return with bags full of tourist stuff. We had flipped that. We left the ship laden with bags and returned with nothing. Each time we did this, they looked more bemused than the time before. Bags are only searched on return, not when you get off, so they had no idea that we were taking all the food and drinks we could carry to local families. When we went up to breakfast one morning, Christian asked one of the waiters what would happen to all the food that was left over at the end of a meal. The waiter told us that it would be thrown away. Christian was horrified because on the day before, we had seen some children who looked very hungry standing at the end of a dock. We asked the waiter how much of the food we could have. He seemed a little put out by the question, "You Americans, you eat big. You eat more than a herd of cows!"

"Actually, we don't want it for ourselves," I explained as I tried to stifle a laugh. "We thought we might take some off the ship to some of the local people."

Well! He became like Robin Hood and wrapped it up in to-go boxes for us with a fervor that would have made Richard the

Lionheart proud. All morning, we conducted our little covert operation. We felt like Brother Andrew sneaking Bibles into China!

As I reflected on that experience, I realized that the barrier that exists on a cruise ship between the passengers who have paid a lot to be there and the crew who often work for minimum wage and send every cent home to their families was breached for a moment by a common desire to taste a little justice and mercy on this earth.

As the waiter worked with my family that day, for just a moment, I felt as if we were one family. Labels and uniforms often divide us, but underneath we are all flesh and blood with hopes, dreams, and disappointments, longing for even a few moments that make sense, that seem right in a world where so much is wrong.

Roll Over and Laugh a Lot

Our next cruise was to Alaska. It was a breathtaking experience. The scenery was magnificent as fjords and lakes, glaciers and mountains spread out before us as we sailed through its icy waters. The highlight for us was the day we went dog-sledding. Christian, Barry, and I were taken by helicopter to one of the great glaciers where for six months of every year there is a two-hundred-dog camp set up at the top.

We all wrapped up like Nanook of the North, and as we stepped off the helicopter onto the snow, I thought again how blessed Christian is to see the things he sees and visit the places he visits as a child. The lead musher escorted us to our pack of dogs to get acquainted. One of the dogs had recently given birth to six puppies, and Christian was given one of the furry bundles to hold.

After we had toured the camp, we were ready to set off. Barry and I got into the sled and tucked Christian in between us. Our musher yelled something that sounded like "Hike!" and we were off. What a blast! The dogs took off across the snow like the Polar Express. The pure joy of it made me laugh out loud. After our first run, the musher asked Christian if he would like to lead the pack. He responded, "Yes, ma'am!"

She said to him, "All you have to remember is, hold on tight, have fun, and if you fall off, roll over and laugh a lot!"

Sounds like a life motto to me!

Eureka!

My mother, Betty, was with us for our cruise in 2005. She still lives in the same small town in Scotland where I grew up but has been able to fly over and join us for each of our cruises—thank the Lord for frequent-flyer miles! As we boarded the ship in Boston, all I could think about was how much work I had to do. I was working on this manuscript and a new children's book, *Gigi, God's Little Princess*. And as is typical every summer, I was in the middle of our busiest time at Women of Faith because we have conferences every weekend.

I brought my computer on board, hoping that sometime between our meetings, spending time with Barry and my mom, and playing ping-pong with Christian I might be able to write a few intelligible sentences. On conference weekends, we have anything from twelve to twenty thousand women with us for two days, but on a ship we have about six hundred women for a week, so there are more opportunities to get to know each other at a deeper level. There were three women in particular whom I spent some time with, and each touched me deeply as I thought about our struggle to be Wonder Women. One was dealing with painful events in her childhood and her relationship with her father. One was suffering with depression after her husband had walked out and left her and their children. One was dealing with being single and a deep familiar loneliness.

I sat on deck one night, watching the moon paint a ribbon of orange light across the water and thought about their stories. I was praying for each one and the difficult circumstances they were dealing with when my "Eureka!" moment came to me: we're in the wrong nest! That's why everything feels so wrong, that's why we don't like the reflection we see in the mirror, that's why we experience such intense loneliness at times. Like the ugly duckling, we were born in the wrong nest.

A Parable

Now, before you think I have gone off on some ornithological rabbit trail, let me try to explain what I mean with a little help from Hans Christian Andersen. When God created Adam and Eve, I want you to imagine that He made them as beautiful swans.

They were graceful and elegant; every move seemed effortless as they swam side by side. When they gazed at their reflection, they saw just what they expected to see, beauty and perfection. Eden was the perfect nest for swans. It offered everything a swan could ever need.

But one day a water serpent approached the swans and spoke of more. He urged them to reach out and taste this untried fruit. As they did, it was as if an earthquake rumbled beneath the lake, and the still water was churned up, splashing their feathers, throwing debris across their path, great waves coming between them. They tried to hide what they had done from the Swan Keeper, but no matter how hard they tried, they could not make the surface of the water smooth like a sea of glass anymore. The Swan Keeper told them that they could no longer live in Eden—they were banished.

As they made their way across the dusty earth, their feathers became all brown and matted. The first time that the female swan looked at her own reflection in a pool of water she was shaken. No longer beautiful and white, she did not recognize herself; nothing was familiar anymore. Whereas she had once swum side by side with her mate, now they often pecked at each other or swam alone.

When she knew that she would have a little one, she did all she could to recreate the nest of Eden, but no matter how hard she tried, it didn't look like a swan's nest at all.

She thought about what the Swan Keeper had told her before they left Eden's lake, "From your eggs will come a Swan Deliverer."

She wondered, "Will it be from this egg?"

When that first little egg cracked and the baby struggled to break free of any remnants of shell, the swans held their breath. When they saw their little one, they couldn't look at each other. All semblance of swan was gone. They had given birth to quite an ugly duckling. The little duck grew, and as he learned to swim and play, he often thought of those first days and wondered why his mother would swim off alone, pecking at her own feathers. Then there was a new egg in the nest. By now, the swans understood that there would be no cygnets, and so they welcomed the next baby duck.

The first duckling never quite forgave them and came to resent this newcomer whose welcome seemed so much more effusive than his own. A small, hard rock grew inside him, and he nursed it every day until the only thing left to do was to kill this quiet intruder. He would punish them all.

As the mother swan swam alone that night, both ducklings gone, one dead and one banished, she wept.

The Wrong Nest

Eve had no way of knowing how long we would have to wait for our Deliverer. One day, we will look in that sea of glass and discover that indeed we are swans again after all. But until then, we struggle with our reflection, with our feathers, with our environment. We think that if we do enough no one will notice the color of our feathers. Our daily challenge is to remember that what we now see reflected back at us in the mirror is only temporary. We used to be swans, but instead of a snowy white coat, we wear one that is brown and rough. We were made for more, and when we were displaced from Eden and turned out into this earth, there was no way that we could ever feel at home.

When Jesus came, He offered to take our filth onto His snowy white back and let us rest under His feathers so that when the Father looks at us, He sees us as we were always meant to be—swans!

Jesus sees us as we really are and loves and welcomes us to come to Him. He offers to clean out our closets and fill them with garments to keep us safe and warm until we see the Swan Deliverer, face-to-face.

> Then I saw a new heaven and a new earth. The first heaven and the first earth had disappeared, and there was no sea anymore. And I saw the holy city, the New Jerusalem, coming down out of heaven from God. It was prepared like a bride dressed for her husband. And I heard a loud voice from the throne, saying, "Now God's presence is with people, and he will live with them, and they will be his people. God himself will be with them and will be their God. He will wipe away every tear from their eyes, and there will be no more death, sadness, crying, or pain, because all the old ways are gone."
> —Revelation 21:1–4 (NCV)

A Look in the Mirror

What do you believe God sees when He looks at you?

How do you identify with the Ugly Duckling?

Can you make peace with who you are until we see Jesus face-to-face?

A Closet Prayer

Father God,

Thank You that You sent a Redeemer into this world to cover my sin and restore my soul. I thank You that I can take shelter under His wings until I see You face-to-face.

Amen.

Part Three

*New Clothes for
a Wonderful Woman*

Sixteen

A Straw Hat:
I will change the way I think

For as he thinks in his heart, so is he.
—PROVERBS 23:7 (NKJV)

*"Just because I'm paranoid doesn't mean
they're not out to get me."*
—WOODY ALLEN (b.1935)

It was a beautiful, fresh June morning, and as the sun shone through our den windows, I suddenly saw how dirty they were. Our new home is in a rapidly developing area. Across the street from us, five homes are being built, so I am constantly dusting the furniture and sweeping sand and construction site debris off the front porch. But it was only as the rays of the rising sun moved across the glass that I realized how much of the grime had adhered to our windows after the last big rainstorm.

I love home do-it-yourself projects, so I hunted through my supplies in the garage until I found what I was looking for. I attached the bottle of window cleaning liquid for outdoor use, to the end of my garden hose and got busy. After getting every window nice and soapy, I hosed them down with fresh, clean water and stood back to admire my handiwork. They looked awful. They looked worse now than before I started. Instead of a thin film of grime across the entire pane of glass, now there were streaks of muddy water running down each one as if my amateur efforts had brought them to tears.

I decided that what I needed was a squeegee, a wonderful tool designed to go over each pane of glass and wipe the water off. I had a similar thing for the shower, so I took the stepladder out and got to work on each window. That did not help one bit. As the sun finished off the drying process, I still saw streaks everywhere.

Next, I got my bottle of regular Windex and paper towels and polished each pane of glass one by one. By the time I finished, and the windows did not look much better, I was totally frustrated. I raised a white flag, admitted defeat, and called a window cleaner.

He told me that he could come the following day. I was relieved as my mom was arriving from Scotland in two days, and I didn't want her to see the house for the first time looking like a flock of geese had thrown up over north Dallas.

He said he would be there by 11 AM, but there was still no sign of him by noon. I was about to call when the phone rang, "Hi, this is your window cleaner."

"Hi, I was just wondering where you were."

"I'm dehydrated."

"Excuse me?"

"I'm dehydrated from my first job, so I'll have to go home and get something to drink."

"I can give you something to drink."

"I need a clean shirt."

"Oh."

"I will be there by one."

"Okay." One o'clock came and went as did two, three, four, and five. At six, he called.

"I thought if I could lie down for a few minutes, it might help, but I fell asleep. I thought if I did fall asleep, I would wake up in a little while. Dehydration must make you very tired, I think."

The Hypothermic Gardener

My mother lives in a small stone cottage in Ayr on the west coast of Scotland, on the very street she was raised as a child. It is a charming home with a pretty front yard and a small patio at the back. The location is perfect as she is five minutes away from my sister's home and ten minutes away from church and the ocean.

There is not much to be done in the way of gardening, but even what there is has become too much for her. Osteoporosis runs in our family, and Mom has three fractures in her spine already. None of the women in our family started out very tall and we seem destined to end our days as garden gnomes.

One early summer morning, two young men came to her front door advertising their services as gardeners. Mom was happy to employ them. The grass had already been cut, so all she needed them to do was weed the flower beds and edge the grass. They declared that would be no trouble at all. It should have taken an hour at most, but they possessed the gift of stretching things out. Five minutes after they began, the doorbell rang again—they needed to borrow tools. Mom opened the garden shed and let them have what they needed. Five more minutes passed, "Could I have a glass of water?"

Then at five-minute intervals: "Do you have a bandage? I've cut my finger." . . . "Could you show me which ones are weeds and which ones are flowers?" . . . "When you say you want the grass edged, what do you mean by 'edged'?"

Then the ultimate: "Is there a drugstore near by? I think I have hypothermia." (This condition is not normally associated with temperatures in the 70s!)

The problem with my window cleaner and Mom's gardeners is that what they *thought* did not match with reality. The window cleaner thought that if he just relaxed for a short while, he would feel better, and if he fell asleep, he thought he would wake up in time. When neither of these thoughts produced the expected results, he thought it might be because he was dehydrated. Having used him one more time, I can tell you that he is stuck in unreliable thought patterns. The next, and last, time he didn't show up because he thought it might rain. Let me just say that there was not a cloud in the sky.

Mom's gardeners' misconceptions were more basic—they thought they were gardeners!

How We Think Affects How We Live

The above may seem like a very basic statement, but even if we acknowledge its truth, I think we often underestimate its implications for our lives. If you think that you are a failure in some area of your life, it may be your thought patterns that are keeping you in a rut; too easily, you accept defeat. Take something as basic and frustrating as dieting—familiar to most women!

How many times have you started a new diet on a Monday morning convinced that this is the time you will beat the reluctant last ten pounds, or you begin a bigger weight-loss plan and succeed for a while only to fail a few days later? If you are like me, you then spend the next few days beating yourself up and eating like your life depended on it. Self-condemning familiar thoughts reenter the picture and take the place of our initial hopes. Too often these thoughts are cruel: *I'll never do this. I am a failure. I knew this would happen. I am so pathetic. What's wrong with me?*

How Do You See Yourself?

During a lunch break at one of our conferences, my friends and I decided to play a little game. We had to describe three things that we liked about ourselves. It was very interesting as it showed how we see ourselves. Mary Graham, the President of Women of Faith, was hilarious! She saw her three strengths as, "I can swallow a lot of vitamins at one time, I don't need a lot of sleep, and I don't have a sweet tooth."

Those things may well be true, but they are by no means Mary's greatest strengths. She is one of the most gifted leaders I have ever met, but she is by nature a humble leader and doesn't always see the giftedness that those of us who love her and work with her see.

She is not the kind of person who would ever push herself forward, but as God has promoted her over and over, I have watched her walk in line with God's estimation of her character and ability. By lining her own mind and heart up with God's call, she is able to shine at what she does. If you asked Mary if she feels capable of leading the largest women's conference ministry in the world, I know she would say no. But rather than look at where she might feel inadequate or give way to self-doubt, Mary chooses to live each day in who God says she is, knowing that if she is about to take a wrong turn, God will redirect her steps.

> Your ears shall hear a word behind you, saying,
> "This is the way, walk in it,"
> Whenever you turn to the right hand
> Or whenever you turn to the left. —Isaiah 30:21 (NKJV)

This verse is a wonderful promise from God that if we have committed our lives to Him and want to honor Him with our lives, He will direct our paths. You might not feel adequate for the place that God has placed you, but our adequacy is not the issue. If God has called you, He will give you everything you need. What goes on under our straw hats affects everything about our lives.

The time to worry is when you think you know exactly what you are doing and can handle everything yourself. Unreliable thought processes not only hinder us in being able to do the job God has called us to do but also trip us up in who God has made us to be.

A Scottish Sage

> O wad some Power the giftie gie us
> To see oursels as ithers see us!
> It wad frae mony a blunder free us,
> An' foolish notion.[1]

Scottish poet Robert Burns only lived for thirty-seven years, but during his short lifespan he was a prolific writer. He wrote about life and love, hypocrisy and human failings, of which he had many. He often attacked the Church for our lack of love and mercy toward those who openly struggle with sin. The above is one of his most oft-quoted stanzas. He wrote it in church one morning as he watched a small louse crawling on the hat of the lady in front of him. The issue here was not what was going on under her hat but what was taking place on top of it!

The poem is called "To a Louse." The first seven verses are addressed directly to this ambitious little crawler, but the final stanza is a prayer. Roughly translated it says: If only God would give us the gift of seeing ourselves as others see us, it would free us from many mistakes and inflated ideas of who we are and what we can accomplish.

I have grateful empathy for much of Burns's writing. He and I came from the same town, and I take great pride in owning him as Scotland's greatest poet, but I part company with him on this thought. What we need to live by is not what other people think of us but who God says we are. Others view us through broken glass; only God has a crystal-clear view. We see each other through the distorted pieces of our own experience, our failings, insecurities, and jealousies. If we want to change the way we think, we need God's help. When Paul wrote to the church in Rome, he made this appeal to our brothers and sisters there:

> Don't copy the behavior and customs of this world, but let God transform you into a new person by changing the way you think. Then you will know what God wants you to do, and you will know how good and pleasing and perfect his will really is. —Romans 12:2 (NLT)

The Greek word used for *transform* is *metamorphoo,* which translates literally "change, transfigure, metamorphosis." Only God can do this, but we can help. When we become believers, our transition from the kingdom of darkness to the kingdom of light happens in an instant, but the transformation of our hearts and minds is a process. We can choose to dwell on what our culture tells us that real beauty looks like, or we can use the mirror of God's Word as a more accurate reflection.

Wonder Woman's value is rooted in what she does, but a wonderful woman's worth is based on who God says she is. What Wonder Woman views in her mirror is often discouraging, but we are offered another mirror. I came to understand this more fully through my new friend, Jennifer Rothschild.

Lessons Learned in the Dark

At the age of fifteen, Jennifer was diagnosed with a rare, degenerative eye disease that would eventually plunge her into a world of total darkness. Her dreams of becoming a commercial artist and cartoonist faded as she wrestled with practical questions: *How will I finish school? Will anyone want to marry me? How will I put makeup on or do my hair?*

Jennifer joined us for eight conferences in 2005. She is quite an amazing woman. Unless you saw her walk in with the help of her husband, Philip, or a girlfriend, you would not know that Jennifer is blind. There is no cloudiness in her big brown eyes, and she turns and looks at you when she is talking to you, and her eyes seem to dance. She maneuvers a large platform with comfort and grace, using four rugs that tell her where she is at any given moment. As a team, we were struck by her humor and giftedness, but there was one thing that Jennifer shared in her message that I will never forget.

Tips for a Bad Hair Day

A friend had given Jennifer some new eye pencils and lip liners, carefully separated so that she would not confuse them. Jennifer's mom had kept her promise to her daughter that she could wear makeup when she turned sixteen. Even though when she made the promise she had no idea that her daughter would be blind, she taught Jennifer how many times to brush her blush brush across the palette before applying it to her cheekbones and how to apply lipstick and eye makeup. Jennifer told us that it's a foolproof system unless she loses count. One day she was getting ready to speak at a woman's event and was struggling with her hair. She said, "You might think that one of the advantages of being blind is that you can't tell when you are having a bad hair day, but let me tell you, ugly has texture!"

Having struggled all she could and still feeling out of sorts with her hair, she decided to try her new lip and eyeliners. When it was time to leave, she went into the den to say goodbye to one of her boys who was playing a video game. He briefly looked up and said to her, "Mom, your lips are black."

To which she replied, "You're just not used to seeing me with lip liner. This is called raisin berry."

Her son went back to his game. Jennifer heard Philip in the garage and went out to meet him. When he saw her, he cried out, "Jennifer Rothschild, your eyes are flaming red!"

Obviously, she had mixed up the lip and eyeliners. She assured our audience that if they are ever having a bad hair day, put eyeliner on your lips and lip liner on your eyes, and there is not a soul in the world who will notice your hair!

Even as we laughed at her vulnerable story, she moved into our hearts when she told us that she has only one mirror in which she can see herself. The only mirror available to Jennifer Rothschild is the mirror of God's Word. Those of us with human sight look in mirrors every day. We see the little lines and grey hair. We see unwanted pounds or tired eyes. We view ourselves critically as we compare ourselves to what our society says beautiful looks like.

Let me stop here and ask you to reflect for a moment. When you look in a mirror, what do you see? What are the things that your eyes gravitate toward? How critical are you when you look at yourself? What are the tapes that play over and over in your head?

Jennifer told us that the only mirror available to her is the mirror of God's Word. When she looks there she sees:

You made my whole being;
   you formed me in my mother's body;
I praise you because you made me in an amazing
   and wonderful way.
   What you have done is wonderful.
   I know this very well.
You saw my bones being formed
   as I took shape in my mother's body.
When I was put together there,
   you saw my body as it was formed.
All the days planned for me
   were written in your book
   before I was one day old.
   —Psalm 139:13–16 (NCV)

Jennifer is comforted by the truth that even on a day when she feels alone, she knows that God is always thinking about her, and His thoughts are amazing.

Let all those who seek You rejoice and be glad in You;
Let such as love Your salvation say continually,
"The LORD be magnified!"
But I *am* poor and needy;
Yet the LORD thinks upon me.
You *are* my help and my deliverer;
Do not delay, O my God. —Psalm 40:16–17 (NKJV)

For I know the thoughts that I think toward you, says the LORD, thoughts of peace and not of evil, to give you a future and a hope. —Jeremiah 29:11 (NKJV)

Always on My Mind

It's quite something when you sit with that truth for a while. The God of the universe, who holds everything together, who is sovereign over every ruler on the earth is thinking about you. Our president has the people of the United States of America on his mind on a daily basis. Occasionally, some are granted the privilege of a personal meeting and a few exchanged words; then, it is time to move on. It is unlikely that as the president goes to sleep each night he is thinking of everyone he met that day, never mind the millions that he has never met.

But God our Father is thinking about us every day. When God thinks about us, His thoughts are 100 percent accurate. He doesn't think we are smarter than we are or less able than we are. He doesn't think we are as godly as the image we try to present at times when we are feeling spiritual or dismiss us as hopeless wretches when that is how we feel. God knows all that is true and loves us totally. So we don't struggle with what God thinks; we struggle with what we think.

God's Word never changes. He always sees us as beautiful and amazing; it is we who change as the world around us changes. Our challenge is to keep the image of the woman God sees more prominent than the image of the woman we see with our human eyes. The new hat that God offers for our wardrobe represents putting on His truth every time we look in our human mirror.

If Eve had never sinned, do you think that every woman born would have been beautiful by our standards? We can never know that. All I can be sure of is that no matter how we looked on the outside, we would have seen each other with our hearts, and a heart in perfect fellowship with God is beautiful. If we are to live as wonderful women in this world, our call is to change how we think about our lives.

Perhaps the greatest challenge of all is to guard our hearts, for it is out of the heart that all the issues of life flow. We are most in danger when our hearts are not fully engaged in relationship with God. When we are not passionate in our life with Him, we look for something else to give ourselves to. We will look at this more closely in the next chapter.

A Look in the Mirror

When you feel overwhelmed, where does your thought process take you?

What is your most common negative thought about yourself?

How could you counter that with the Word of God?

Write out a scripture that will help you line up your heart with God's truth when you are tempted to fall back into old unhealthy patterns of thought.

A Closet Prayer

Father God,

Thank You that You are always thinking about me. Thank You that Your thoughts toward me are always good and loving and merciful. Help me to line my thoughts up with Your Word.

In Jesus' name,
Amen.

Seventeen

A Strand of Pearls:
I will guard my heart

Keep your heart with all diligence,
For out of it spring the issues of life.
—PROVERBS 4:23 (NKJV)

"Stay away from the light!"
"But it's so beautiful!"
—*A BUG'S LIFE,* PIXAR FILMS (1998)

I believe that when God has our heart, really has it, when there is nothing in life more important than serving and loving Him, only then do we feel really alive. Many women are simply bored with their lives. It's not a lack of activity that is the problem but a lack of passion.

We were made to be fully alive, engaged, committed, and when we are not, we can get into all sorts of trouble. We can lose ourselves in activity and become the Wonder Woman on our book cover. Busyness is not the same as passion. We can also lose heart altogether. We can find our hearts engaged where they don't belong.

God has not left us alone or ill-advised in this situation. Scripture is full of parables and stories that address the very real needs that you and I face today. God is talking to us all the time if we have ears to hear Him.

Revelation!

I experienced that recently as I began a study on the second and third chapters of Revelation given to John on the Isle of Patmos. Here, Christ is addressing the angels of the seven churches in Asia Minor. Most theologians agree that Christ is referring to literal angels whose charge it is to watch over the believers in a particular city. Those churches may seem irrelevant to where you are in your life today, but as I looked at what Christ had to say to each one, God spoke to me.

In each of the seven situations, the issues presented are issues of the heart. When the church addressed is in a good place, it is because of their passion for Christ. When they are in danger of sin, it is because their hearts have either become cold or engaged elsewhere.

This is our story, and even if we are separated from John's vision by two thousand years, the struggles and temptations that our brothers and sisters encountered then are with us still today. The truth contained in each situation is a gift to wrap around our hearts like a strand of perfect pearls. Each pearl is perfectly made for a wonderful woman.

First Love Lost

God accused the angel of the church in Ephesus of leaving their first love. They were busy doing all the right things, but their hearts were not in what they were doing. Ephesus was the most important city in Asia Minor at that time. It was almost a New York of its day, a big city with big money changing hands as fortunes rose and fell. It was also the center for worship of the goddess Artemis or Diana.

Because it was such a strategic city, Paul had given almost three years of his life to help establish the church there. The potential for the believers in Ephesus to influence their world and culture was enormous. But now Christ brought their offense to light.

Although their activities were still intact, their hearts had lost their passion. Does this sound familiar? God wants more than our time and our efforts; He wants us. He wants us to be fully engaged with Him in the matter of living and loving rather than just ticking jobs off a long to-do list. I wonder how many of our churches have become just like those in Ephesus. The hallmarks are easy to recognize. The church is busy, even successful, but there is no joy, no warmth, and no passion for Christ and for one another; the heart is not engaged. True to the grace and mercy of God, the warning comes with a promise that takes us right back to the Garden of Eden: "To him who overcomes I will give to eat from the tree of life, which is in the midst of the Paradise of God" (Rev. 2:7 NKJV).

In this divine pep talk, I hear a clear wake-up call to remember whose we are. It is clear from verse seven that we can overcome mere slavery to duty.

If you find yourself in a place where you look back with regret and wonder where your first love has gone, don't give up, don't ever give up! No matter how faint our desire is to change or how weak our resolve, if we will come to our Father as we are and ask Him to rekindle our hearts with fire for Him, He will do it. Jesus says, "So remember where you were before you fell. Change your hearts and do what you did at first" (Rev. 2:5 NCV). This one verse is a key to rekindling love of any sort. It applies in our relationship with Christ or with our husbands. Those three ingredients can change even the coldest of hearts.

1. *Remember where you were.* Remember what it was that made

you fall in love at first. Was it the way God reached out to you and you felt truly loved for the first time? Was it the overwhelming truth that your sins could be forgiven and you could be given a new start? The same holds true in your relationship with your husband—what was it that made your heart beat just a little faster every time you saw him and made you want to do all those little things that you knew would mean the world to him?

2. *Change your heart.* Open your heart to being vulnerable and open again. Lift up your head and say—Yes!

3. *Do what you did at first.* What was your life like when you first met Christ? Did you devour your Bible, look for times to be alone with the Lord, tell others about your love for Him? Don't wait until you *feel* like it; *act* like it, and the feelings will follow.

This life that we cling to and try to squeeze every ounce of satisfaction out of is nothing compared to the life that waits for us in heaven when once more we will be invited to feast from the tree of life. But while we are still on this side of the Garden wall, we can, by God's grace, rekindle our hearts to burn for Him.

Purified by Pain

Thirty-five miles to the north of Ephesus was Smyrna, a busy seaport, and another church Christ addresses in Revelation. The church in Smyrna, having already experienced some persecution, was on the verge of experiencing even more. Christ warns that some of them will be thrown in prison but encourages them to take heart, not to be afraid, for He is with them. Many of the believers in Smyrna are poor, and it seems from the text that they are being persecuted by the large Jewish community, presumably those who don't accept Christ as the promised Messiah. Even as they are warned of the upcoming period of persecution, Jesus reminds them that to those who endure will be given the crown of life. This was a significant term to a Greek culture that lauded athletes and awarded each winner with a garland, or crown, to celebrate their victory. Such a reward is promised to those who bear all things for the sake of Christ. Christ Himself will celebrate their victory!

It's interesting to note throughout Church history that persecution has often been the strange friend of the believer. When the heat was turned up and a choice had to be made, time after time, we see the Church stood strong even when it cost everything that this world holds dear.

The Cost of the Rope

I was moved recently after reading about three nineteenth-century Korean workmen who had a heart to take the gospel to their country. Most of us are aware of the amazing growth of Christianity in South Korea in our time, but I had no idea that the fruit we now see had been watered more than a century earlier by the blood of faithful men and women.

In his book, *What in the World Is God Doing?*, Dr. Ted Engstrom of World Vision relates a story he heard from a veteran Korean Christian. He writes that in the early 1880s, three Korean workmen laboring in China heard the gospel and gave their lives to Christ. Their mission became a commitment to get the Word of God into their own country, an act forbidden by the government. Since the Korean and Chinese alphabets were similar, they decided to smuggle in a copy of the Chinese Bible. They drew straws to see who would have the privilege of bringing the gospel into Korea even though they knew that it could cost them their lives.

The first man buried the Bible in his belongings and headed toward the border. There he was found out and killed. Word reached the others that their friend was dead. The second man tore pages from his Bible and hid the separate pages throughout his luggage. He, too, made the long trip to the border only to have his belongings searched, and be found out, and beheaded.

The third man grew more determined than ever to succeed. He ingeniously tore his Bible apart page by page, folding each page into a tiny strip. He wove the strips into a rope and wrapped his baggage in his homemade rope. When he came to the border, the guards asked him to unwrap his belongings. Finding nothing amiss, they admitted him.

The man arrived home, untied the rope, and ironed out each page. He reassembled his Bible and began to preach Christ wherever he went. And when the missionaries of the 1880s and 90s fanned into the country, they found the seed already sown and the first fruits appearing.[1]

I am humbled by the faith and commitment of such believers. I would never be brave enough to pray that I might be persecuted, particularly since I am a mom, but I do see that when assaults come against God's people, they tend to purify our hearts and clarify our vision. I believe that although we would never seek it, should persecution come to us, Christ will sustain us.

Persecution comes in many forms. It can be the relentless onslaught of chemotherapy or poverty or difficult relationships. The very things that could push us far away from God, when offered to Him, can be the sweet ropes that tie us close to His heart.

The Danger of Concession

The next church Christ addresses is the church in Pergamos, the ancient capital of Asia, fifty miles north of Smyrna. This body of believers had allowed some of the habits and practices of their culture to infiltrate their lives, even though they went contrary to God's Word. Some ate food that had been offered to idols, and some were involved in inappropriate sexual behavior.

It must have seemed easy to justify using food that had been offered to idols. The food was there, the animals had already been slaughtered, so wasn't it better to use it than to waste it? Some couples lived together even though they were not married, and again I can hear the argument, "But we are committed to each other; we are as good as engaged. We're not promiscuous; we are faithful to each other."

That vast grey area of justification and negotiation has always been there. Compromise can easily be confused with grace, but they are not the same. I have talked with many young Christian women who are single and sexually active. I have listened as they have explained that they are being faithful in one relationship and intend to marry, which they reason is so much better than many of their friends who are openly promiscuous. But sin is sin, no matter what shade of grey we color it.

As our culture becomes increasingly tolerant, Christians can easily be infected without even realizing it. I have to be so careful about what movies I take Christian to see. Even if the movie we are scheduled to watch is okay, there is no guarantee that the trailers for upcoming movies will be acceptable.

I am a huge poster girl for grace. We all are at Women of Faith. At times we are openly criticized because we don't publicly address hot issues such as abortion or homosexuality. Our response to those who feel we don't take full advantage of our platform is that the call God has placed on us as a team is to communicate the love and mercy of God, to say, "Come as you are, and be welcomed into His family."

God is more than able to speak to each one of us individually about our lives once we are in His arms. I will always hold that to be true, but as I study this warning to the church at Pergamos, I find myself chastened to bring my own life under the scrutiny of the Holy Spirit and ask Him to show me where I have used the truth of the grace of God as an excuse to grow comfortable in areas that I should show caution. I have no heart to be a goody-two-shoes, but I do want to be a godly woman. I want my heart to be a place where God is pleased to dwell.

There is an analogy woven throughout Scripture that compares food offered to idols and promiscuity. It began with the children of Israel wandering in the wilderness and is seen here in Pergamos as well. I don't know what the modern equivalent of food offered to idols would be (perhaps tithing your gambling winnings!), but the central message is clear: it is compromise. The promise offered to those who would resist compromise: "I will give some of the hidden manna to everyone who wins the victory. I will also give to each one who wins the victory a white stone with a new name written on it" (Rev. 2:17 NCV).

The hidden manna refers to a feast to be shared with Christ that would make any other meal pale by comparison. The *white stone* was a familiar term to those in Pergamos. It was something that was awarded to athletes or gladiators for completing unusual feats of bravery; often, the giving of the white stone meant that they could now rest from battle.

The bottom line I see here is *don't settle,* but press on for what God's best is. That is a pearl worth treasuring.

A City Set on a Hill

The Spirit now moves to address the church at Thyatira, thirty miles southeast of Pergamos. Thyatira boasted a large military base, so the church there had an opportunity to impact an audience that spread out to a wider geographical area. There are many things about the church there that Christ commended—their patience and charity, their growth in faith and wisdom—but the complaint against them centers on the character Jezebel.

Theologians disagree as to whether this is one woman named Jezebel, or a comparison Christ is drawing between the church at Thyatira and the Jezebel Elijah encountered in the book of First Kings, or even a name for a group of women so alike in spirit and deed that they are grouped together under this title. *The New King James Commentary* describes her as a believer who is under God's discipline but who will not repent and change her ways. Posing as a prophetess, she is sexually immoral and deceptive. Matthew Henry, in his commentary on Revelation, offers no such hope for Jezebel's future repentance:

> I will cast her into a bed, into a bed of pain, not of pleasure, into a bed of flames; and those who have sinned with her shall suffer with her; but this may yet be prevented by their repentance. I will kill her children with death; that is, the second death, which does the work effectually, and leaves no hope of future life, no resurrection for those that are killed by the second death, but only to shame and everlasting contempt.[2]

Whatever the truth is about Jezebel, why is this church, which is commended by Christ in so many areas, held responsible for her behavior? Matthew Henry writes that God accuses this church of allowing this woman's influence to taint their city, perhaps even members of the church and of the military community as well.

The Church, however, had no civil power. They could hardly put an immoral woman under citizen's arrest. So I wonder if the challenge to the church at Thyatira, and to us, is Jesus' teaching in Matthew 5:13–16:

"You are the salt of the earth; but if the salt loses its flavor, how shall it be seasoned? It is then good for nothing but to be thrown out and trampled underfoot by men.

"You are the light of the world. A city that is set on a hill cannot be hidden.

"Nor do they light a lamp and put it under a basket, but on a lampstand, and it gives light to all who are in the house.

"Let your light so shine before men, that they may see your good works and glorify your Father in heaven. (NKJV)

I am not a big fan of protest marches or anti-anything campaigns, but I am a huge cheerleader for the Church shining so brightly in the community that others are drawn to Jesus. In my experience, most nonbelievers are aware that they do not have all their ducks in a row. When we come after them with a long list of everything that is wrong with them in our view, that spirit gives birth to animosity, and, more often than not, they will point fingers back at our own hypocrisy and lack of love. We are called to live in our culture with pure hearts, fully engaged in loving Jesus, and sharing His grace and mercy at every possible opportunity.

A Long Obedience in the Same Direction

The church at Sardis was in a desperate situation, and to make matters more treacherous, they seemed unaware of their position. They had a reputation for being a lively growing community but they were dead and lifeless. They started projects and didn't finish them because their hearts were apathetic.

Walking faithfully with Christ year after year takes vigilant commitment. It's not easy to keep doing the right things over and over. It's no walk in the park to keep on loving, keep on forgiving, keep on serving, but that is what we are called to do as the Church.

Those in Sardis had become tired and were now simply going through the motions. Paul warns us of this same pitfall in his letter to the Galatians, "We must not become tired of doing good. We will receive our harvest of eternal life at the right time if we do not give up" (Gal. 6:9 NCV).

You Shine!

The church in Philadelphia is shown, in contrast, as one that has persevered. Even though they don't have much strength or position in this wealthy city, they have remained faithful, and there is nothing but praise for them. What a great place to be in! That's what I want to hear from the Lord, and I'm sure you do too. Isn't it so easy to get caught up in things that don't matter and let the real issue of life, loving and serving God, take a back seat? God's Word to the church in Philadelphia is to remember that Christ is coming back soon. When they become discouraged, they are called to refocus on the truth that there will come a day when every human trial and test will be over, and they will stand before the throne and worship the Lamb forever.

I don't know how you envision heaven, but when I was a young girl, I used to think it sounded deadly boring. I mean, how many rounds of "Kumbaya" can one sing? I believe my early ideas were so wrong. Heaven will be what we were always made for. Randy Alcorn has written a wonderful book called *Heaven*, published by Tyndale Press. You may not agree with everything he writes about heaven as some things, he admits, are supposition based on the limited description given in God's Word, but he gives a marvelous picture of the glorious life that is waiting for us.

Sometimes we need a bigger picture than what we are experiencing at this moment—don't lose sight of who you are and where you are headed. When we lose sight of the bigger picture and become ensnared by the issues and love of this world, we can find ourselves in the situation of this last church.

Don't Believe Your Own Press

The church in Laodicia made God sick—this is a strong statement but accurate: "So then, because you are lukewarm, and neither cold nor hot, I will vomit you out of My mouth" (Rev. 3:16 NKJV).

There is more involved here than just a church that has lost its first love. There is a smug deception involved: "You say, 'I am rich, have become wealthy, and have need of nothing'—and do not know that you are wretched, miserable, poor, blind, and naked" (Rev. 3:17 NKJV).

They had come to a place in life where they didn't even realize that God was no longer in the picture of their lives. Laodicia could be compared to a city like Boston. It was a city of banks, rich in textiles, and the proud parent of a large medical school. They thought they were in a great place, but they were not. Lukewarm water is of no use to anyone. In their community, cold water was refreshing, and hot water was medicinal, but lukewarm water served no purpose. It looked the same but proved useless.

So, too, in the offering of our spiritual lives to God. It's scary to think that you could be part of a church that you believe God is really blessing because it's growing, and all events are well attended, but in reality, the pervading spirit is like warm soup. I have a pet peeve with soup that tastes like it's been sitting out for twenty minutes before it was served. It represents to me a meal that has not been thoughtfully watched over. If you have ever been served a meal like that, you feel like saying, "Why did you bother?"

God wants our hearts fully engaged as we offer the feast of our lives to Him. You are worth that! There is no joy in offering less than the best. It neither blesses the giver nor the one who receives.

She Who Has an Ear to Hear, Let Her Hear

God wants our hearts. He doesn't want our activity alone, our busyness, our long list of things we have done for Him; He wants us. I am still amazed by this, but I hold it to be the dearest truth of my life that the God of the universe wants my heart. No matter what our culture, or at times the Church, tells us about what really matters, this truth remains: God loves us, and it is His driving passion to be loved by us. You were made for nothing less. May the truth of these pearls wrap around your heart. You are a wonderful woman!

A Look in the Mirror

As you reflect on your life, what are the things that make your heart beat faster because you are engaged and passionate about them?

To which of the seven churches do you most relate?

How can you rekindle your first love for God?

A Closet Prayer

Father God,

Thank You that You want more than my days, You want my heart. I ask that by the power of Your Holy Spirit You would rekindle, or light for the first time, a flame that would burn for You and You alone.

In Jesus' name,
Amen.

Eighteen

A Chair in the Corner:

I will make a place to feed my spirit

> *Look, the Lord GOD is coming with power*
>   *to rule all the people.*
> *Look, he will bring reward for his people;*
>   *he will have their payment with him.*
> *He takes care of his people like a shepherd.*
>   *He gathers them like lambs in his arms*
>   *and carries them close to him.*
> *He gently leads the mothers of the lambs.*
>
> —ISAIAH 40:10–11 (NCV)

> *Solitude is sweet.*
>
> —WILLIAM COWPER (1731–1800), "RETIREMENT"

How much time do you spend alone? Now, if you are a mother of three, finding ten minutes to read a few lines in your own private sanctuary (the one that flushes!), you may be laughing out loud right now.

If you are a working woman who comes home late, cooks a quick meal, sticks some laundry in the washer, and falls into bed, you might consider laughing tomorrow as you are far too tired to muster up even a chuckle tonight.

If you are a busy wife, involved in your church and your women's group, grabbing enough groceries on the way home to see the family through the weekend, alone time for you might be the time you spend stuck in traffic.

We are not a culture that embraces solitude. We live in a world of noise and activity and then wonder why it is so hard to sleep at night or to experience the ongoing peace that Christ promises to those who love Him. We equate being alone with loneliness and shun it whenever possible, but alone time was a high priority for Christ. He took time away from the crowd even though they clamored for more. He often walked away from those who still had needs, problems, and sicknesses to be alone with His Father. If this was a priority for Jesus, we are foolish to ignore the pattern of His life.

> Immediately Jesus told his followers to get into the boat and go ahead of him across the lake. He stayed there to send the people home. After he had sent them away, he went by himself up into the hills to pray. It was late, and Jesus was there alone. —Matthew 14:22–23 (NCV)

A Prepared Life

I truly believe that one of the most important lessons I am learning at the moment is the call to spend some alone time with God in the midst of the rush of my life. Christ knew that His times were in the Father's hands. He knew that He was about to walk through the darkest night a human being will ever experience, and it was in His times of quiet communion with His Father that He received the grace and strength for what was to come. He made a place in His inner closet to sit with His Father and be still.

Wonder Woman has no time to be alone. She is far too busy saving the world, but a wonderful woman knows who she is *because* of the time she spends alone with her Father.

Think about your life for a moment. Are you anxious about anything? What are the thoughts that typically run through your head as you rush from thing to thing? When was the last time you found a quiet spot to sit for a while and do nothing but enjoy being there (without falling asleep!)? Are you facing a dark and difficult time in your life?

It is not enough to simply remove activity from our Wonder Woman existence. We have to replace it with something better. We are invited to fill the void with the intentional habits of a wonderful woman.

Christ has promised you and me that we can live in this world with its constant change and threats, from within and without, and know His perfect peace.

> "I leave you peace; my peace I give you. I do not give it to you as the world does. So don't let your hearts be troubled or afraid." —John 14:27 (NCV)

> "I told you these things so that you can have peace in me. In this world you will have trouble, but be brave! I have defeated the world." —John 16:33 (NCV)

Paul, a man facing great difficulties, who would eventually give his life for the sake of Christ, wrote to the church in Philippi with a prescription for peace:

> Do not worry about anything, but pray and ask God for everything you need, always giving thanks. And God's peace, which

is so great we cannot understand it, will keep your hearts and minds in Christ Jesus. —Philippians 4:6–7 (NCV)

Paul wrote those profound words under the inspiration of the Holy Spirit, and those God-breathed words had become habits that Paul embraced. He could not have faced the persecution and imprisonments he endured with such grace and strength otherwise. Paul was a man who made time and space in his life to sit quietly with God and feed his spirit.

Often it takes a crisis to reveal to us how hungry our spirits are. Paul's words are gifts to us so that when we find ourselves in a desperate place, our spirits won't be starved.

So Far Away

Does the peace that Christ promises and Paul wrote of seem a million miles away from the circumstances of your life today? As a nation, we are at a record high in the consumption of drugs for anxiety, depression, and compulsive thought disorders. Many of us cannot sleep at night without the help of either prescribed sleeping pills or an over-the-counter version.

As I have written, I take medication for depression and am very grateful for it, but what you don't know is that up until fairly recently, I took something to help me sleep every night. Like most of you, I lead a very busy life. When I am on the road with Women of Faith, our schedule is pretty hectic. For thirty weekends a year, we live in hotel rooms. I try to make our room feel a little more like home and less like a sterile unfamiliar place, but it is still a hotel with strange noises and under-stuffed pillows. (I always seem to get the pillow where the down was donated by a duck with alopecia!) On Friday nights, when I get back to my room after our evening event, I find it hard to unwind. Knowing that I have to be up early the next morning, I got into the habit of taking an over-the-counter sleep medication.

Barry asked me one night, "How often do you take those?"

"Every night," I told him.

"I don't think that's good for you," he said.

As I thought about my life patterns, I saw the way that I had allowed myself to get squeezed into the mold of how our culture lives. I drink too much coffee to wake up and take pills to get to sleep.

I asked God to help me break some of those patterns. For the first few nights, I had a hard time falling asleep, but I decided not to worry about it. I kept a flashlight by the bed and read my Bible or a good book until I got sleepy. I soon discovered that I woke up earlier and was not nearly so groggy.

Some of you may be taking sleep meds, and I have no desire or right to comment on the choices you make for yourself. I just wanted to let you know that since I stopped taking mine, I feel more alert. Our world offers us pills to fall asleep and pills to wake us up. It offers pills to alleviate anxiety and to lift our moods.

Some of these are necessary for the broken world we live in, but I think we have become too dependent on those and not enough on the presence of the Great Healer and Peacemaker. We get to choose each day how we will feed our spirits. Being alone and quiet in the presence of God is one of the greatest feasts you will ever experience. So, too, is time with the Word of God.

I said to the man who stood at the Gate of the Year,
"Give me a light that I may tread safely into the unknown."
And he replied, "Go into the darkness and put your hand into the hand of God.
That shall be to you better than light and safer than a known way!"[1]

A Quiet Time to Read

I enjoy studying. I love the process of digging deep into a subject that I know very little about and gleaning from the wisdom of those whose life's work has been to unpack its mysteries.

I discovered when I went to graduate school in the fall of 1993, however, that there is a right way to study and a wrong way. Graduate school papers have to be presented in a certain layout, either using *The Chicago Manual of Style* or a similar style guide. I had no idea that such a thing existed, but had I heard the phrase dropped in conversation I would have assumed it had to do with how to accessorize a suit.

My first class in seminary was in church history. I scanned the list of possible research topics as Professor Nathan Feldmeth explained the requirements of the paper. The paper had to be twenty-five pages long and include a bibliography of reference material with the appropriate footnotes and endnotes. He ended by telling us, "Fifty percent of your grade will be based on your research paper, which must be turned in two weeks before the end of the semester."

Fifty percent! For the next few nights, I sat at my desk at home and wrestled with the task of writing this paper. I didn't know what a footnote or an endnote was. A footnote sounded like a "P.S." and I thought an endnote might be the "Amen!"

I had imagined that all I had to do was write the paper and have it typed up so that it was neat with no telltale signs of coffee spilled on the pages and no bits chewed by Abigail, my cat. I realized that I was in over my head.

After the next class, I asked the professor if I could talk to him.

"I don't know how to do this," I admitted.

"What do you mean?" he asked kindly.

"Well, I've never written a paper for a graduate class, and I honestly don't know where to start."

For thirty minutes, Nate sat with me and went over each step: how to research, how to catalog the research, how the finished paper should look. He helped me to understand how to access knowledge, how to read a book so that I will understand it, grasp hold of what is being said, and then determine if I agree with the writer. I left that meeting grateful for his guidance and guidelines. I felt less ignorant, more confident that I could take one step at a time. I was also deeply grateful to God for setting me free from the fear of asking for help or admitting that I needed it.

Liberated by Truth

I have discovered that study is a faithful friend if we learn its ways. I see that a great deal of damage is done, not by evil, but by ignorance. Christ tells us that we will know the truth and the truth will set us free (John 8:32), but so often we don't know what the truth is. We don't know how to dig it out.

In Romans, Paul tells us that our lives are to be transformed by the renewing of our minds. But if we have no firm grasp on what God's Word says, how can we be changed by it? You will know the truth, and the truth will set you free, but first, you have to know it!

There is nothing in life more important than understanding God's truth and being changed by it. God has given us a mind so that we can learn and grow. As His people, we have a great responsibility and wonderful privilege of growing in our understanding of Him.

I like to take a passage of Scripture or a good Christian book and write down what strikes me or what questions I have as I read. When

I get together with my friends, I'll throw these thoughts into the arena, and we'll wrestle with them to grasp hold of what God is saying to us. When we dig deep, there are hidden treasures to be found.

> Your Word is like a flaming sword
> A sharp and mighty arrow
> A wedge that cleaves the rock;
> That word can pierce through heart and marrow
> Oh, send it forth o'er all the earth
> To purge unrighteous leaven
> And cleanse our hearts for heaven.[2]

You Are What You Eat

Each day we choose what we are going to feed our spirits, our souls, and our minds. We choose how to balance it, and our lives testify to what we are taking in. With food, we are told that we are what we eat, and that would hold true for spiritual food too.

When we feast on what's on the news and what arrives in the mail, what phone calls we receive or what negative thought patterns keep reoccurring, it should be no surprise that fear, anxiety, and sadness show up in our lives. Our Father has an alternate menu for the child of God: a mainstay of hearty meals on the Word of God seasoned with prayer.

A Divine Menu Plan

Breakfast

> LORD, every morning you hear my voice.
> Every morning, I tell you what I need,
> and I wait for your answer. —Psalm 5:3 (NCV)

But I will sing about your strength.
>In the morning I will sing about your love.
You are my defender,
>my place of safety in times of trouble. —Psalm 59:16 (NCV)

Fill us with your love every morning.
>Then we will sing and rejoice all our lives. —Psalm 90:14 (NCV)

We petition, we sing our praises, and we are filled with the love of God!

Lunch

Happy are those who don't listen to the wicked, . . .
They love the LORD's teachings,
>and they think about those teachings day and night.
—Psalm 1:1–2 (NCV)

Guide me in your truth,
>and teach me, my God, my Savior.
>I trust you all day long. —Psalm 25:5 (NCV)

I am always praising you;
>all day long I honor you. —Psalm 71:8 (NCV)

I will meditate on the Word of God; I will trust Him and sing His praises.

Dinner

I praise the LORD because he advises me.
>Even at night, I feel his leading. —Psalm 16:7 (NCV)

The LORD shows his true love every day.
>At night I have a song,
>and I pray to my living God.
—Psalm 42:8 (NCV)

LORD, I remember you at night,
  and I will obey your teachings. —Psalm 119:55 (NCV)

In the middle of the night, I get up to thank you
  because your laws are right. —Psalm 119:62 (NCV)

I will thank God and rest in the promise that He is leading me. I will sing and pray, remembering to choose to do the things that honor Him, and when I can't sleep, I will get up and thank Him all over again!

Sounds like a menu fit for the daughter of a King! It sounds like the kind of feast enjoyed daily by a wonderful woman.

A Look in the Mirror

What do you think it is that is difficult about being quiet?

Where could you begin to carve some alone time into your day?

What is your spiritual diet like every day?

Do you know that you have an all-you-can-eat pass to the banquet of God?

A Closet Prayer

Father God,

Thank You that You sent Jesus to this earth to show me how to live. Teach me to be quiet and to feast on Your love and grace every day.

In Jesus' name,
Amen.

Nineteen

Running Shoes:

I will honor my body

So I tell you, don't worry about the food or drink you need to live, or about the clothes you need for your body. Life is more than food, and the body is more than clothes. Look at the birds in the air. They don't plant or harvest or store food in barns, but your heavenly Father feeds them. And you know that you are worth much more than the birds. You cannot add any time to your life by worrying about it.

—MATTHEW 6:25–27 (NCV)

I am actually a perfect size 10; I just keep it covered with fat so that it doesn't get scratched.

—BARBARA JOHNSON (b.1927)

By the time Jesus sat down and began to teach, the crowd was large. He had traveled all over Syria, and as He moved from town to town teaching and healing people, many left their homes and followed Him. They had never seen anything like this before. They experienced new emotions as they listened to this man talk and watched Him gently interact with those who were bruised and broken by life.

It seemed as if heaven had kissed earth, and for a moment people who hadn't spoken to one another in a while looked at each other and smiled. There was grace where there had been no grace.

When Jesus sat down, they hurried to get a good seat, knowing that whenever a rabbi sat, he was about to teach. It was hard to fully understand what He said, for it was as though He spoke in riddles, but they pushed in closer to hear.

"What did He say?" a woman asked her husband.

"He said that we should be happy if we know that we are poor in spirit."

"Why?" she asked.

"I don't know, Martha. Be quiet now, I just missed a bit."

On and on Jesus taught. Those who are sad now are happy because God will comfort them. Those who are humble are happy because the earth will belong to them.

That night as Martha and Simon lay in bed she said, "I didn't understand much about what He said today, Simon, but I loved to listen to His voice. It's the kind of voice that you know will never steer you wrong. I liked the bit about not worrying . . . now that Miriam's wedding is so close. That's all she thinks about these days . . . 'What will I wear, Mom? What will I put in my hair?' I wish she had been there today, Simon. Simon? Simon? Are you listening to me?"

But Simon was fast asleep, far away on a boat somewhere catching enormous fish.

Don't Worry, Be Happy

I wonder if there is any teaching of Christ that is more difficult for a woman to follow than this: don't worry about the food or drink you need to live, or about the clothes you need for your body. Boy, do we struggle with this! Think for a moment about the time and money you have lost consumed with thoughts about what you are going to eat or not eat and what you are going to wear. More than any other area in my life, I have wasted time worrying about what I look like. I could just slap myself with a large fish for being so foolish! But in 2005, I made a huge breakthrough, and I don't think I will ever go back to how I used to live.

Before I get to that, let me give you a little personal history. Perhaps you will find yourself in my story.

The Butcher's Scales

My friend Moira and I gazed at the pictures of the models in our new magazine. A school friend had brought it back from a trip to America, and we were fascinated. Toward the end of the magazine, there was a chart that gave the correct weight range for every height. I had no idea that such a thing existed.

"How tall are you, Moira?" I asked.

"Five feet, two and a bit inches," she said.

"Okay, well you should weigh between one hundred and one hundred and twenty pounds if we don't count the wee bit," I said.

"How much is that?" she asked.

In Scotland, we weighed in stones and pounds. (There are fourteen pounds in each stone.) I took out my calculator from my school bag.

"That's between 7 stone 2 pounds and 8 stone 8 pounds," I said. "That's quite a margin."

"How tall are you?" Moira asked.

"I am five feet, four inches. What do I get to weigh?"

She studied the chart. "You should be between one hundred and twenty pounds and one hundred and thirty-five pounds. That's between 8:8 and 9:9. What do you weigh?" she asked me.

"I have no idea. What about you?"

"Me either," she said. "We don't have scales at home. Where do you think we could find some?"

"I know!" I said. "Let's ask the butcher—he has to weigh cows, he must be able to handle us."

The butcher was very accommodating and let us slip into the back of his shop and weigh ourselves. Moira discovered that she was just where she should have been at one hundred and nine pounds. I, on the other hand, weighed in at one hundred and forty-two pounds.

"Good grief!" I said. "I'm half a cow!"

And So It Begins

I wonder if you can remember the first time that you realized that you exceeded the supposed ideal for your weight. I know that some of you reading this will never have struggled with weight issues or may even have battled being underweight, but for the majority of women in our culture, weight is a huge issue—no pun intended.

When I left the butcher's shop that day, I saw myself as I never had before. I saw myself as a fat girl even though the previous day I had weighed the same amount and felt just fine about myself. I asked my mom at dinner that night why she had never told me that I was fat. She told me that I wasn't fat, I was just growing. "Yes, but in what direction?" I wanted to know.

No Limits on the Limits

In Scotland at that time, if you wanted to lose weight quickly, our drugstores carried a brand of meal substitutes called Limits. They were disgusting big cookies that tasted like raffia coasters. I duly went and bought some, and for the next few days, I had them for lunch and dinner. At the end of a week, I had lost three pounds and was developing quite a friendship with the butcher! I plodded on for another week 'til five pounds were gone. By then, I felt I had consumed enough fiber to sink a ship, so I quit my very first diet. Little did I know then how many times I would relive that experience.

You name it, I've done it: Weight Watchers, Jenny Craig, LA Weight Loss, Atkins, Slim Fast, the Cabbage Soup diet . . . and on and on!

Weight Watchers is a very good program, but I got bored and discouraged that I didn't lose twenty pounds in the first week—my expectations were a shade unrealistic back then.

Jenny Craig works well for many, but as I travel so much, it's hard to heat the prepackaged food in a hotel room over a candle, and trust me, I've tried! Even after I quit, the counselor kept calling, trying to encourage me to get back on. Barry would say, "It's the Jenny Craig police on the line. They've tracked you down."

LA Weight Loss worked very well for me for a time until I came off to celebrate my birthday and could never quite get back on again. I have a warped mindset when it comes to diets. I think, *Well, I tried that once, and it didn't work, so I need a new plan.*

Ah, the mystery and allure of a new plan! It never crossed my mind that the diets worked; it's just me that didn't.

If I Eat One More Egg, I Will Self-Combust

When the Atkins diet hit big, I was sure that I had found the answer to all my prayers. Now I could officially go to the Waffle House for breakfast! I would order a cheese omelet and crispy bacon, coffee and cream. I could eat hamburgers and cheese and steak, and I could tell that I was losing weight quickly. I did fine for about two weeks, and then I hit my maximum protein intake limit—MPIL!

No, that is not a scientific term; it's just a reality I faced as I found myself staring at a plate of meat and imagining it walking around in a field with me chasing it with a knife and fork. Some seem to do well on this program for months, but I could not, not on the Slim Fast program or on the Cabbage Soup diet either. There is only so much cabbage one person can eat before turning an interesting shade of green.

I will spare you the blow-by-blow walk through my twenties, thirties, and forties and simply sum it all up with a comment my pastor made one day, "Sheila, if you just carried all your diet books up and down the stairs a few times, you wouldn't have a problem."

God Honored Here

If I could hang a sign around my neck to indicate that I am a believer, I'd want it to read: God Honored Here. I have realized for years, however, that when I am consumed by how I look and what diet I am on or off, "God Honored Here" would not be an accurate statement. More than the waste of money, I regret the time I have wasted in self-punishing cycles. Instead of having on internal running shoes that would take me to a healthy place of honoring God with my body, I kept going in self-defeating circles.

I see it in the lives of my friends and family too. As I began to write this book, I knew that one of the big issues for Wonder Woman is how she looks to others, and I wanted to be free from that compulsion. As I prayed for God to help me find victory to live free from these endless cycles, one phrase kept coming to me over and over again: a long obedience in the same direction, which is also the title of a book by Eugene Peterson that I read many years ago. This phrase captures the heart of what it actually looks like to put on your running shoes and honor God every day in your body.

A Long Obedience in the Same Direction

Over the years, I have been asked several times to write a diet book, and I have resisted strongly for two reasons. One, I never stayed on one long enough to have any credibility, and, two, I didn't want to use a God-given platform to sell to such an emotional issue for women. God has given me the honor of having input into the lives of hundreds of thousands of women, and I consider that a sacred trust not to be taken lightly. But I am happy to pass on what I have learned this year as I do believe it would make a difference in everyone's life.

No Fool this Time

On April 11, 2005, I weighed myself—148 pounds. I decided that day to begin a healthy-eating program that included lean protein and good carbohydrates, such as fruits, vegetables, and whole grains. My commitment was simply that, to keep taking the next step toward a healthier body and not look back or be ruled by the scales. I weighed myself once a week. The first week I lost the most weight, which is to be expected. After that, some weeks I didn't lose much at all, but I didn't allow myself to dwell on being discouraged; I just kept going. A long obedience in the same direction!

By August 1, I was at my goal of 125 pounds. I have to tell you that I feel better than I have in years. The biggest lesson that I have learned is simple—most good-eating plans work if they are consistently followed. I could have achieved the same results on many of the plans I mentioned above if I had continued to follow the program.

I had to decide what I really wanted to do with my body. Did I want to indulge it every time the mood hit me, or did I want to bring my desires under the lordship of Christ? Did I want a healthier body to serve Him well for as long as I could?

To tell you the truth, sometimes I just want to indulge myself and probably always will, but more than that, I want to honor God with my life. Many in the evangelical community frown on those who consume alcohol or smoke cigarettes, but we are guiltier of overindulging in food that can lead to tremendous health problems. I'm sure you've heard the phrase, "Where two or three are gathered in Jesus' name, there will be a casserole in the midst."

I hope you can hear my heart through my story. The purpose of writing this is not to say that there is a right size or weight to be or to suggest that those who are thinner are honoring God more than those who are overweight—far from it! Being thin is a god in our culture; that is not what I am aiming for. What I want in my life and for you is a life in balance, where the only god worshipped is God alone.

When I joined a gym recently and was asked what I wanted to accomplish, I said, "I want to have a strong body to serve God as well as I can for as long as I can." I wish I had taken a camera—my request was obviously not in their manual! We live in a culture that encourages us to be thin and healthy for our own sakes. I believe that the call of a wonderful woman is to be strong and at peace, to be able to love God with everything she has and love others with unencumbered abandon. We have the privilege of consciously putting on our running shoes every day. By that I mean, shoes don't just slip on themselves, we have to bend down and do it. So, too, with honoring the Lord with our bodies. It won't just happen. We have to get up every day and mentally put on those shoes and say, *Today, Lord, this is one more day where I will take a long obedience in the same direction.*

You can do it, wonderful woman!

A Look in the Mirror

In what ways has your body image dominated your thoughts? Has weight or dress size become a god in your life?

Jesus said, "So I tell you, don't worry about the food or drink you need to live, or about the clothes you need for your body." What changes can you bring in your life to let go of worry and stress?

A Closet Prayer

Dear Father,

I want to honor You in my body and in my mind. Please help me to live a long obedience in the right direction.

In Jesus' name,
Amen.

Twenty

High Heels or Flip-Flops:
I will celebrate who God made me

You changed my sorrow into dancing.
You took away my clothes of sadness,
and clothed me in happiness.

—PSALM 30:11 (NCV)

Follow your own path and let people talk.

—DANTE (1265–1321)

I am writing this chapter with a parrot on my head. Yesterday, I didn't own a parrot, but today, not only do I own one but she also thinks that she owns me. I never intended to have a parrot . . . but then I never intended to have a green tree frog either, and somehow one led to the other with brief consideration for a leopard gecko. It was an act of God that moved the heart of my husband to say that Christian could have a frog.

Frogs, Lizards, and Parrots . . . Oh, My!

When Christian turned eight in December 2004, one of the girls in his class gave him a Grow Your Own Frog kit. Inside the box was a

193

small tank and a certificate to send off for your tadpole, which we did, and it arrived ten days later. Finnie, as Christian named him, did well for about a week, and then one morning, we discovered that he was either sunbathing or dead, floating on his back. When Barry saw how upset Christian was, he agreed to a small frog.

"I want one that made it all the way, Dad."

As we drove off to the local pet store, Barry's words were ringing in my ears, "Get a small one, so small that I don't even know it's in the house!"

The Great Plagues of Egypt

Christian picked out a frog with bright emerald skin and we asked a store assistant what else we might need.

"We have a small tank that came with our tadpole," I told her. "Will that do for the frog?"

"No!" she said, barely concealing her horror at my ignorance. "You will need a ten-gallon tank."

"Ten gallons? How big is this thing going to get?" I asked.

"It's fully grown now, but you need room for the lights and the waterfall," she said.

I looked around for the cameras to see if I was on some comedy show.

"Waterfall . . . what exactly do you mean when you say . . . waterfall?" I asked.

"The frog needs constantly running water, a UVA light, UVB light, and a night light. He would also enjoy a hammock," she added.

"Wouldn't we all!" I said. She didn't seem amused.

"Where do you keep the cans of food?" I asked.

"They don't come in cans," she said.

"What doesn't come in cans?"

"Live crickets."

As I drove home with a happy boy, a huge tank, and two of the great plagues of Egypt in the backseat of my car, I thought, *I wonder if this is what Barry had in mind.*

Freddie did well for several months, and then, one morning when I went to mist him down (don't ask!), I saw that he was out of the tank, sitting beside it, and dead. I don't know how he got out, but Christian was very upset. I found a jewelry box and put Freddie in it surrounded by fresh flowers. My mom, sister, and brother-in-law were staying with us, so they were invited to the viewing. Ian, my brother-in-law, declined, so I told Christian he was probably too upset, which I'm thankful he bought. After the funeral, we talked about who could take Freddie's place. Barry had always said that he would consider most small pets but never a lizard.

The Lizard

"Should we get another frog?" I asked Barry. "I know that a lizard is out of the question."

"He can have a lizard," he said. "Can you find a non-slimy one?"

I bought *Lizards for Dummies* and began the non-slimy search. We settled on a leopard gecko as it is easy to handle, doesn't grow to be eight feet long, and is non-slimy. Barry decided that he would come with us this time. We visited four pet stores and looked at all they had to offer. In the fourth store, we noticed a beautiful bird on a perch and went over to say hello. As we watched it stretch out its wings, Christian said, "I wish we could get a bird."

I said, "I've always wanted a bird."

Barry added, "I love birds!"

We looked at each other in amazement.

"I didn't know that you've always wanted a bird," Barry said.

"Well, growing up Mom hated birds, so I never had it on a list of possible choices," I said.

We went home, got online, and researched birds.

Amazing Grace

Not far from where we live, there is a store called Kookaburra that specializes in birds and bird training. The moment we entered the store, we all fell in love with one bird. She is a Jenday conure, and we named her Grace. So as I sit here at my desk in my home office, Grace is either on my head or on my shoulder. She is very affectionate and loves to cuddle into my neck or watch cartoons with Christian. Barry's favorite expression now is, "Can I hold my bird?"

Who Are You?

One of the greatest joys in life is finding out who God made you to be, with all the personality quirks, and loving it. I have always gathered little animals. Growing up as a child in Scotland, we didn't have much money, so my pets were frogs that I caught in the quarry, or worms that I dug up, or the one mouse that a boy in my class gave me that by the next morning was seven mice! Often when we arrive at adulthood, get married, or settle into a career, we abandon parts of who we are and relegate them to the attic of our mind. I think when we do that, we lose a little piece of ourselves.

Think back to your childhood. What was it that made you unique and special? How were you different from your siblings or your parents? What did you love to do at school? What were the things that you did better than anyone else?

You might be a high-heels girl or a total flip-flop woman. You might love yourself in dresses or only feel at home in jeans. Too often as we grow, we conform too much. Part of conformity is necessary to meet job requirement standards or out of respect for others. Where we lose the wonder of who are, though, is when we conform just to be like others because we are afraid to be different. Different is good!

Luci Swindoll has kept a journal since she was a child and continues to journal into her seventy-third year. Barry has collected house plans and decorating ideas since he was a little boy, and he drags out his file at least once every day. Patsy Clairmont is a Scrabble genius. She loves words and delights in a game that counts on the twenty-six soldiers of the alphabet for its success. Each of us has a unique God-given personality to celebrate.

Wonderfully Made

There is no one else in the whole wide world like you. I'm sure you have heard that before, but I wonder if you understand how true it is and how precious you are to God? We are not always treasured on this earth. Our relationships with our parents or friends or spouses can lead us to believe that we may be unique, but that it's not a good thing. So often we are encouraged to blend in, don't rock the boat, don't be different, but I say, rock that boat, and be who you are.

Max Lucado has written a wonderful book called *Cure for the Common Life*. I highly recommend it. He says that each one of us has what he calls a "sweet spot" where we are meant to live. He writes, "Stand at the intersection of your affections and successes and find your uniqueness."[1]

When you hold back who you really are, we all miss out. So whether you are a pet nut like me or a wordsmith like Patsy, whether you like high heels or flip-flops, be who you really are. You have a voice and a style that is all your own. It has been given to you by God so that through you, a unique picture of our Father is seen:

But you are a chosen people, royal priests, a holy nation, a people for God's own possession. You were chosen to tell about the wonderful acts of God, who called you out of darkness into his wonderful light. —1 Peter 2:9 (NCV)

A Look in the Mirror

As you look back over your life, what are the personality traits that were there as a child that you have suppressed as an adult?

What are your unique gifts?

Do you value how God has made you or wish you were like someone else?

What is your "sweet spot?"

A Closet Prayer

Father,

I thank You that You have made me unique with gifts and abilities that You placed in my life alone. Help me by the power of the Holy Spirit to identify those and offer them to You.

In Jesus' name,
Amen.

Twenty One

Regular Hose:

I will let God be in control

I look up to the hills,
but where does my help come from?
My help comes from the LORD,
who made heaven and earth.
He will not let you be defeated.
He who guards you never sleeps.
He who guards Israel
never rests or sleeps.
The LORD *guards you.*
The LORD *is the shade that protects you from the sun.*
The sun cannot hurt you during the day,
and the moon cannot hurt you at night.
The LORD *will protect you from all dangers;*
he will guard your life.
The LORD *will guard you as you come and go,*
both now and forever.

—PSALM 121:1–8 (NCV)

'Tis so sweet to trust in Jesus,
And to take Him at His Word;
Just to rest upon His promise,

And to know, "Thus says the Lord!"
Jesus, Jesus, how I trust Him!
How I've proved Him o'er and o'er
Jesus, Jesus, precious Jesus!
O for grace to trust Him more!

—Louisa M. R. Stead (1859–1907)

When I was in my twenties, if I wanted to lose two pounds, I could do it in a week. In my thirties, it took a couple of weeks, but in my forties, it takes spring and most of summer! Our season at Women of Faith runs from March through November, and during that time, I am pretty disciplined with my eating, but when the season is over, I tend to relax and go nuts. (Now, since my big breakthrough in the spring of 2005, I will obviously not do that anymore—*please God!*) At the end of our 2004 season, I let up even more than normal. We flew to Scotland for Christmas, and my family produced every kind of food that I have ever said I liked since I was able to utter a word or butter my own bread.

When I got home and tried on one of my suits, things were not looking good. I decided that the dry cleaners must have shrunk the pants, and it was time to look for a new suit. I took a trip to the mall, found a couple of possibilities in one store, and headed off with hope in my heart to the dressing room. As I looked at myself in a three-way mirror, I was reminded of a quote attributed to Woody Allen: "It's not the despair that gets you, it's the hope!"

Let me just say this, there is no way God ever intended a woman to see that much of herself at one time. Three-way mirrors are clearly a result of the Fall! I was instantly transported back in my mind to wash day in Scotland.

Every Monday, all the housewives would do the weekly wash and hang it outside on the clothesline to dry. As a young girl, I was fascinated by certain items that hung like weapons of warfare. My mother referred to them as control garments. I remember thinking, *What are they trying to control, a herd of Holsteins?* Now, as I gazed at my small herd in the mirror, I knew that the time had come for me to investigate what the new millennium had to offer in the way of undergarment wrangling. My grandmother's words rang in my ears, "Even if you weigh the same when you hit forty as you did at twenty, things will have shifted."

Legs Like an Elephant

As I made my way to the lingerie department, a very enthusiastic sales associate offered to assist me. I explained that I needed some help smoothing out some areas.

"Oh, we have lots of things for you!" she cried, thrilled with her new project.

"I don't want lots of things," I assured her. "Just one thing would be fine."

She produced something that looked like hose with the feet cut off and told me that they were all the latest rage.

"They were on Oprah," she said, lowering her voice to a reverent whisper. "They're called Spanx!"

"Spanx!" I replied with horror in my voice. "I can't wear something called Spanx—I'm a Christian!"

I bought one pair, took them home, and tried them on with one of my suits. At first, I was very impressed. From mid-thigh to my waist, I had a new smooth outline until I looked at my whole body in the mirror and realized that all they had done was move everything north! I headed back to the mall and explained to my enthusiastic friend what had occurred.

"I just knew it!" she cried. "I have lots of other things for you to try."

My next purchase resembled a shell or tank top, but underneath, it had a structure that would rival the Eiffel Tower. When I put it on with the Spanx, I was smooth from my shoulders to my thighs, but I had legs like the Elephant Man.

No Illusion

What I discovered that day was the control offered by lingerie is nothing more than an illusion. It helps the appearance of anything that might have shifted, but it doesn't change anything. I also discovered that one of the best things about control hose is taking them off! It is such a huge relief. So, too, when we take our hands off our life and accept the liberating truth that God is in control.

He is in control, at all times, no matter how things appear to be. I believe that more now than I have at any other point in my life. Perhaps *believe* is not the right word. I understand in the deepest place in my spirit that God is in control and that He loves me. I used to feel at the mercy of circumstances or the whims of others. In my mid-thirties, I experienced a parting of the ways with someone who had been involved with my career for many years, and I believed that person had the power to make sure I never worked in the Christian music world again. That is a terrible place to be. Perhaps you have experienced something similar in your own life.

You know that God has called you to some kind of ministry, then your husband leaves you. Finding yourself divorced, you think that your call is over too.

You are laboring on in your church, and no one seems to notice or care or validate what you are doing.

You have worked for years somewhere, and things have been going really well until a new person comes on the scene who doesn't seem to like you, and you believe that person can ruin you and what God has for you.

Either God is in control all the time, or He is not. God's timing is not always our timing, but He is never one moment too late or too early. We often say as Christians that we understand that God's ways are not our ways, and His thoughts are not our thoughts, but we rarely unpack that truth to see what it might look like.

Shattered Dreams

Think of Joseph. You can read his story in Genesis 37. When Joseph was seventeen years old, God gave him two dreams. In the dreams, his eleven brothers and his mother and father, depicted by eleven stars and the sun and the moon, bowed down before him. His brothers already had little patience with this boy as they watched their father, Jacob, spoil him, but when he shared his dreams and interpretation with them, hatred began to burn in their hearts. When their moment came, they grabbed it and sold Joseph to a traveling band of slave traders headed for Egypt.

What happened to the dream then?

Sold as a slave to a wealthy Egyptian, Joseph soon gained the trust of his owner, who made him head of the estate. Perhaps Joseph thought at that point that, finally, the dreams were beginning to come true. It had taken longer than he thought it would, but now things were beginning to fall into place. Then his master's wife falsely accused him of rape, and he was thrown into prison.

What happened to the dream then?

For at least ten years, Joseph was either a slave or in jail. Did he think he must have misunderstood God? Did he think other human beings had disrupted God's plan for his future? Did he believe that a more powerful person could change his destiny?

When Joseph was finally released from prison, he rose to become prime minister of Egypt and lived to see his brothers bow before him and fall on his mercy.

Two things are very encouraging to me about his story. First, it is clear that no human being can destroy what God has purposed. God's timing is perfect, and His will is perfect.

Second, while Joseph was in the waiting period of over ten long years, he was preparing himself. In the prison system, he was trustworthy and displayed such great organizational skills that he became the warden's agent and ran the prison!

Why, Lord?

Joseph could have sat around in despair for years, wondering where things went wrong, but he didn't. Instead, wherever he was, he used everything that God had placed within him to serve. I have to think that God must have been pleased with Joseph's character and growth. From a headstrong teenager who didn't display much wisdom around his elders, he became a mature, wise, and honored man.

Are You Stuck Right Now?

Perhaps part of your pursuit of Wonder Woman is because you know God has called you to something in particular, and you are doing everything within your power to make it happen. God is not looking for exhausted servants who run around trying to be and do everything in the hopes of being recognized and fulfilled.

Perhaps you have lost heart. You once believed that God had called you, but as time has passed and life has taken a few unexpected left turns, you have simply given up. Loss of hope is a terrible place for the believer to be. I am reminded of Paul's words to the church in Rome, just twenty-five or thirty years after the death and resurrection of Christ:

We also have joy with our troubles, because we know that these troubles produce patience. And patience produces character, and character produces hope. And this hope will never disappoint us, because God has poured out his love to fill our hearts. He gave us his love through the Holy Spirit, whom God has given to us. —Romans 5:3–5 (NCV)

One of the best-known statements from Joseph's life is a glorious declaration of his belief in the sovereignty of God as he addresses his brothers who are finally standing before him, terrified of what he might do to them:

But as for you, you meant evil against me; but God meant it for good, in order to bring it about as it is this day, to save many people alive. —Genesis 50:20 (NKJV)

How Do You Spell Relief?

One of the things I first noticed about Spanx is how great it is to take them off. What a relief! It's the same way with the tight control we try to have on our lives. If we could grasp, by the power of the Holy Spirit, the truth that Joseph embraced, think how it would change our lives.

God is in control, not your husband. God is in control, not your children or parents. God is in control, not your doctor. God is in control, not your boss. God is in control, not a terrorist.

No matter what is going on in your life right now, God loves you and He is in control, so you don't have to try! Take those uncomfortable control-top hose off and breathe a sigh of relief. You are a wonderful woman!

A Look in the Mirror

Does your life feel out of control?

What are the fears that keep you from experiencing the peace of God that Paul wrote of to the church in Rome?

Do you believe that someone else has altered God's plan for your life?

Are you ready to believe that God is in control, no matter what seems to be true?

A Closet Prayer

Father God,

Thank You that You are in control of all things at all times. Help me in my unbelief and fear. I choose to trust You, and even in a time of waiting, I will live with all my heart for You rather than waiting for my life to change.

In Jesus' name,
Amen.

What a Wonder:
I will dare to dream again

To fight for the right without question or pause . . .

—Joe Darion, "The Impossible Dream," *Man of La Mancha*

A wise woman strengthens her family,
but a foolish woman destroys hers by what she does.
Those who respect the Lord *will have security,*
and their children will be protected.
Respect for the Lord *gives life.*
It is like a fountain that can save people from death.

—Proverbs 14:1, 26–27 (NCV)

"Do you know what my favorite two things about you are, Mom?" Christian asked me one day.

"I don't think I do," I said. "Is it my cooking?"

"No, but I do love your penne pasta."

"Is it my jokes?" I asked.

"Definitely not!" he said.

"Well, what then?" I asked, my feelings slightly wounded from the joke thing.

"I love that you love me, and I love your personality," he said.

"That is so sweet, Christian, thank you. What do you like about my personality?"

"I like that you love your life, Mom, and I get to be in it."

I thought about that for a while. My son's comments touched me deeply. I knew, too, that they had not always been true. For many years, I just got through my life. It's really only in the last ten or twelve years that I have loved it, and I have felt so grateful to be alive.

Like Dorothy and her friends as they traveled to the Emerald City, I have been changed by the journey. What once would have terrified me no longer holds that power. It's not that I have become a stronger person, but I know where I am going, and I know who is with me. I know that at every twist and turn of the road, Christ will be there, and because of that fact alone, I am not afraid.

We are all on a journey in this life; we have no choice on that front, but we are either growing or shrinking inside. We are either becoming more fully the woman that God knows us to be or becoming less recognizable daily. Like Eve, we will one day be given the gift of beholding Jesus face-to-face and eating freely from the tree of life, but what about now? The tree is guarded until then, but Jesus has promised living water to sustain us until that day.

> On the last and most important day of the feast Jesus stood up and said in a loud voice, "Let anyone who is thirsty come to me and drink. If anyone believes in me, rivers of living water will flow out from that person's heart, as the Scripture says." —John 7:37–38 (NCV)

Are you thirsty? Are you tired of trying so hard? Jesus invites you to come and drink deeply of His heart, His passion, His joy, His peace.

I have had the joy of watching God transform others from the desperate efforts of Wonder Woman to the rest and peace of a wonderful woman of God. I think of Susan.

A Desperate Housewife

Each year when our team visits Philadelphia, I get an opportunity to catch up on Susan's life. The first time we met, she was standing in my book line with tears rolling down her cheeks.

"I want so much to be a better wife and mother. I'm trying so hard, but I never measure up," she said. "I listen to you tell stories about your son, and I want to have those kinds of stories to tell. I want to be a more consistent mother, but I get mad and lose my temper when he makes a mess or breaks something."

"I am far from a perfect mom," I said. "Just ask Barry and Christian. I make my share of mistakes too. You need to forgive yourself and lighten up a little bit. I'm sure if I talked to your son, he would have wonderful things to tell me about you."

I gave her a hug and my e-mail address, and we promised to keep in touch, but after the first couple of notes, I wouldn't hear from her until the following year. Once more, we would go through her long internal list of every place in life that she perceived herself to be a failure. After the third year of listening to her beat herself up, I asked her to do something for me.

I asked her to write down the messages she received as a child; how did she remember her childhood? When I read her list, it was clear why she had no grace to extend to herself. She was constantly told to do better, be better, or perform better. I made a new list for her and asked her to read it whenever the old tapes played again in her head:

> Yes, I have loved you with an everlasting love;
> Therefore with lovingkindness I have drawn you.
> —Jeremiah 31:3 (NKJV)

How precious also are Your thoughts to me, O God!

How great is the sum of them!

If I should count them, they would be more in number than
the sand;

When I awake, I am still with You. —Psalm 139:17–18 (NKJV)

I will be glad and rejoice in your love,
because you saw my suffering;
you knew my troubles.
You have not handed me over to my enemies
but have set me in a safe place. —Psalm 31:7–8 (NCV)

This is real love. It is not that we loved God, but that he loved
us and sent his Son as a sacrifice to take away our sins.
—1 John 4:10 (NLT)

And I am convinced that nothing can ever separate us from
his love. Death can't, and life can't. The angels can't, and the
demons can't. Our fears for today, our worries about tomorrow, and even the powers of hell can't keep God's love away.

Whether we are high above the sky or in the deepest ocean,
nothing in all creation will ever be able to separate us from
the love of God that is revealed in Christ Jesus our Lord.
—Romans 8:38–39 (NLT)

Susan humored me and said that every time she felt overwhelmed
or condemned, she would try and remember to read one of these
verses. The next time I saw her, I was truly moved by the change in
her countenance. I asked her what the year had been like for her. She
told me that at first, nothing changed apart from her promise to me
that she would read this new list over and over.

"You didn't promise to read it," I reminded her. "You only said that you would try."

"Same thing!" she said with a grin.

She went on to tell me that as weeks turned to months, she realized that she felt a little different inside, not so desperate and intense. She told me that she took my advice and stopped trying to save the world and started letting Jesus save her.

The Whole Point

I think that's the whole point. You and I are not the good news—Jesus is. You and I can't save ourselves or our families; Jesus does that. We can spend the rest of our lives beating ourselves up for being human or accept that Jesus loves and receives us in our humanity. There is something so beautiful about being with someone who understands deep in their spirits that they are loved by God. We want to be around people like that even if we are not there yet. Take a man like Jonathan Edwards, the great American revival preacher.

Full of Joy

Jonathan Edwards is known for many things. His sermon series, *Sinners in the Hands of an Angry God,* preached in 1741, was the beginning of a great spiritual awakening on the East Coast. He was an intense, studious man who enrolled at Yale when he was not quite thirteen years of age. By twenty-one he had earned his master's degree from Yale. He was regarded as moody and stiff, but then he met Sarah Pierrepont. When he met her, she was just thirteen years old. This at-times morose man could think of nothing but Sarah. He scribbled on the cover of one of his books,

Sarah goes from place to place, singing sweetly, full of joy. She loves to be alone, walking in the fields and groves, and seems to have someone invisible always conversing with her.[1]

He married her when she was seventeen. What was it about Sarah that so captured his heart? I think it was the freedom that Sarah knew in her relationship with Christ. She knew that Jesus loved her, and it was a source of constant joy. She didn't try to make everyone like her; it was enough that Jesus did.

Her liberty and pure joy caused a lot of controversy in the churches that her husband pastored. Her freedom was too much for those who were suspicious of grace, but to Jonathan, she was captivating. In Puritan times, they believed that a baby was born on the same day of the week that it was conceived. The fact that six of their eleven children were born on a Sunday was shocking to Jonathan's congregation, for what God-fearing couple would have sex on a Sunday? Jonathan died as a relatively young man due to a smallpox vaccination, but his last message sent to Sarah said,

Give my love to my dear wife, and tell her that the uncommon union which has long subsisted between us has been of such a nature as I trust is spiritual and therefore will continue forever.[2]

If you look at Jonathan and Sarah's descendants you'll find eighty college presidents, professors, and deans; one hundred lawyers; sixty-six physicians; eighty political leaders, including three senators and three governors; and countless preachers and missionaries.

It is rare to find a couple like Jonathan and Sarah. Perhaps as you read his words about her you feel cheated by life. It is possible that you have never felt captivating, but the absolute truth is that Jesus sees you as captivating. As women, we long to be treasured and adored. There is a place within us that was made for that. It is not a vain or foolish thing; it is part of our God-given makeup.

We have looked at Eve's story. She is the only woman who has perfectly tasted what we all long for. As Eve looked at her daughter-in-law's struggles and gazed into the eyes of precious baby granddaughters, there must have been such an ache of regret for what they didn't know and experience. Even there, in the dry desert of our dusty, broken beginnings, there was the promise of the coming Deliverer: "So as one sin of Adam brought the punishment of death to all people, one good act that Christ did makes all people right with God. And that brings true life for all" (Rom. 5:18 NCV).

Time to Dream Again

In this life, we are all packaged differently. We are tall or short, fat or thin, black or white; the differences go on and on. But what we have in common as sisters in Christ should overshadow all of that.

As you are right now, you are passionately loved by God. Jesus is captivated by you. There has never been a moment in your life when God didn't love you . . . not one moment.

You don't have to save anyone, just let Jesus continue to save you. God is in control, so you don't have to try to be. There is nothing that will happen to you today or tomorrow that has not passed through the loving hands of your Father in heaven.

You are not Wonder Woman, but, girl—you are wonderful!!

A Final Prayer

Father,

Thank You that You see me, and You love me. Thank You that to You, I am beautiful and treasured. Today I choose by Your grace to start to really live again and be the woman You have made me to be through the power of Your Spirit and the life and death of my Savior and Lord, Jesus Christ. I declare that because of You, I am a wonderful woman!

In Jesus' name,
Amen.

Endnotes

Chapter 1

1. Sue and Larry Richards, *Every Woman in the Bible*, "Woman in Creation and the Fall" (Nashville, TN: Thomas Nelson, Inc., 1999), 1.
2. Ibid.

Chapter 2

1. John Milton (1608-1674), *Paradise Lost: Book Eight*, line 547; and *Paradise Lost: Book Nine*, line 896.
2. George Herbert (1593-1633), as quoted in *Matthew Henry's Commentary on the Whole Bible* (online edition accessed 10/15/05: http://www.ccel.org/h/henry/mhc2/MHC01002.HTM).
3. George Matheson (1842-1906), as quoted in *All the Women of the Bible* by Herbert Lockyer (Grand Rapids, MI: Zondervan Publishing House, 1967), 57.

Chapter 3

1. Earl D. Radmacher, Ronald B. Allen, H. Wayne House, *The Nelson Study Bible: New King James Version* (Nashville, TN: Thomas Nelson, Inc., 1997).

Chapter 8

1. W. Mackintosh Mackay, as quoted in *All the Women of the Bible* by Herbert Lockyer (Grand Rapids, MI: Zondervan Publishing House, 1967), 23.

2. Nave's Topical Bible Index, NIV Study Bible Complete Library, Zondervan Interactive Software (Grand Rapids, MI: Zondervan Bible Publishing House).

3. Robert J. Morgan, *On This Day*, "The Banner of Jesus" (Nashville, TN: Thomas Nelson, Inc., 1997), June 7.

4. Elizabeth Barrett Browning (1806-1861), "The Sweetest Lives."

Chapter 9

1. Robert Robinson (1735-1790), "Come Thou Fount of Every Blessing" written in 1758; music by John Wyeth.

Chapter 10

1. Harold Begbie, as quoted in *All the Women of the Bible* by Herbert Lockyer (Grand Rapids, MI: Zondervan Publishing House, 1967), 230.

2. Mackay, 230.

Chapter 12

1. "Maria" from *The Sound of Music*, 1965; words by Oscar Hammerstein II (1895-1960).

2. Robert J. Morgan, *Nelson's Complete Book of Stories, Illustrations and Quotes* (Nashville, TN: Thomas Nelson, Inc., 2000), 175.

Chapter 13

1. Hans Christian Andersen (1805-1875), *The Ugly Duckling* (online version accessed 10/28/05: http://hca.gilead.org.il/ugly_duc.html).

2. There was a voluminous amount of religious writing by the time Jesus was born, including those cited in this chapter. In the first two centuries following the birth of Christ, Yose b. Yohanan of Jerusalem was one of the more prolific writers. He wrote primarily about the role of men and women in culture, specifically teaching men to avoid the company of women and so avoid the appearance of evil or the temptation to indulge in evil. These quotations are taken from *Every Woman in the Bible* by

Sue and Larry Richards, "Jesus' Relationships with Women" (Nashville, TN: Thomas Nelson, Inc., 1999), 153.

3. Richards, 156–157.

4. William Cowper (1731-1800), "Heal Us, Emmanuel," *Olney Hymns* (London: W. Oliver, 1779).

Chapter 15

1. Andersen, *The Ugly Duckling*.

Chapter 16

1. Robert Burns (1759-1796), "To a Louse."

Chapter 17

1. Morgan, *On This Day*, "The Homemade Rope" (Nashville, TN: Thomas Nelson, Inc., 1997), July 11.

2. Matthew Henry, as quoted in *Matthew Henry's Commentary on the Whole Bible* (online edition accessed 10/18/05: http://www.ccel.org/h/henry/mhc2/MHC66002.HTM).

Chapter 18

1. Minnie Louise Haskins (1875-1957), quoted by King George VI of England, in a Christmas Broadcast, 12/25/1939.

2. Karl Bernhard Garve (1763-1841), Lutheran minister and hymn writer.

Chapter 20

1. Max Lucado, *Cure for the Common Life* (Nashville, TN: W Publishing Group, 2005), 3.

Epilogue

1. Morgan, *On This Day*, "Never on Sunday" (Nashville, TN: Thomas Nelson, Inc., 1997), July 28.

2. Ibid.

God Is Listening

sheila walsh

best-selling author and women of faith® speaker

get off
your knees &
pray

a woman's guide
to life-changing prayer

Prayer is not just something we *do*—it is who we
are. In *Get Off Your Knees and Pray*, Sheila Walsh
shares the journey of her prayer life and reminds us
of the joy of being in God's presence every day.

THOMAS NELSON
Since 1798

WOMEN OF FAITH®

Best-Selling authors and Women of Faith speakers Patsy Clairmont, Marilyn Meberg, Luci Swindoll, Sheila Walsh, Thelma Wells and dramatist Nicole Johnson bring humor and insight to women's daily lives.

WOMEN OF FAITH